Will
CHINA
FAIL?

JOHN LEE

Will
CHINA
FAIL?

The Limits and Contradictions
of Market Socialism

JOHN LEE

Will China Fail?
by John Lee

Policy Monograph 77

Published September 2007
The Centre for Independent Studies Limited
PO Box 92, St Leonards, NSW 1590
Email: cis@cis.org.au
Website: www.cis.org.au

National Library of Australia
Cataloguing-in-Publication Data:

      Lee, John Cheong Seong.
      Will China fail?– the limits and contradictions
      of market socialism.

      1st ed.
      Includes index.
      ISBN 9781864321807 (pbk.).

      1. Mixed economy - China. 2. China - Economic conditions
      2000- . 3. China - Politics and government - 2002- . I.
      Centre for Independent Studies (Australia). II. Title.

      338.951

©2007 The Centre for Independent Studies
Cover design by Abby French
Edited by Dominic Rolfe
Printed by Ligare Book Printer
Typeset in Adobe Garamond 11pt

CONTENTS

ACKNOWLEDGEMENTS

Enormous thanks are due to Sue Windybank and also Owen Harries for their helpful comments, criticisms and suggestions. I would also like to thank Helen Hughes and Paul Monk for their suggestions, and the two anonymous reviewers of earlier drafts. The responsibility for the work remains my own.

PREFACE

The Centre for Independent Studies has been putting forward ideas that promote the advancement of freedom and prosperity for over three decades. Australia is positioned in the most dynamic region in the world. The most spectacular examples of economic transformation in the last fifty years have occurred in the Asia-Pacific. Recognising that economic freedom and good governance are principles that have brought prosperity throughout many parts of the world including our own, some of our most important work in recent times has had a regional rather than purely Australian focus.

The future of China is the future of one fifth of the world's population. Emerging from the barely imaginable suffering, turmoil and chaos during the Mao Zedong years, hundreds of millions have been delivered from poverty since the beginning of reforms in 1978. China has been growing at enormous pace for almost three decades. Once a 'pariah state' with a backward economy, China (and also India) is emerging as a great power in the region. Building on the Centre's recent emphasis on foreign and particularly regional affairs, this book is our first study of China.

Why does the Centre have a special interest in China? Much of the world's fascination is that China has managed to achieve its 'economic miracle' without dismantling its authoritarian structure - without reforming mechanisms to promote limited government or one that is bound by the rule of law. Courts and other judicial bodies remain under Party supervision, as do the administrative and bureaucratic organs of the state. Significantly, the Party has identified about a dozen key 'strategic' industries and sectors of its economy that it will not relinquish control over – including the financial and banking sectors, hence giving the Party open access to the country's wealth. Not surprisingly, largely inefficient state-owned-enterprises swallow up the bulk of China's capital even as their share of output diminishes. Despite all this, China's economy continues to grow year on year. Moreover where once China was seen as a regional menace most experts are now willing to accept the rhetoric of China's self-termed 'peaceful rise'. China appears to be a 'successful dictatorship' on an unprecedented scale.

For some, China's political structure is irrelevant to its future prospects. For others, including many liberals, growing Chinese economic prosperity will inevitably lead to future political reform; we should therefore continue to support any measures that will further aid its economic growth. To be sure, while we should certainly reject any policies that attempt to contain or inhibit China's economy, we should also be aware that the future of China is much more in Chinese hands than in ours. For this reason, the work of Dr Lee is important as it offers a clearer picture of what is occurring within China, especially the progress of reforms (or lack of them) that are needed to sustain its rise.

Will China Fail? warns against the 'China blindness' that is behind many of our assumptions about China's inevitable 'peaceful rise'. Dr Lee examines the massive economic and social problems within China that many in the West – undoubtedly excited by the lure of a massive market – simply ignore, underestimate, or discount. The book looks at the evidence and presents arguments as to why reform is failing, why much of China's apparent success is illusory and ultimately unsustainable, how its authoritarian political system is squarely behind these problems, and why desperately needed political reform is unlikely to occur in time. Furthermore, Dr Lee makes the case that the future direction of Chinese foreign and security policies remains unpredictable. The logic of peaceful integration into the region – although a powerful one – is competing with a more disruptive one borne out of the regime's opportunism and desperation to remain in power.

Ardently hoping that 1.3 billion Chinese can increasingly enjoy the fruits of prosperity that freedom can bring is one thing. Wishful thinking and false optimism is another. *Will China Fail?* should dispel any complacency we might have regarding the difficulty of China's ongoing transition. Instead, China's system of 'market socialism' is far from a successful contradiction. Its troubles should serve as a reminder of the powerful connection between successful and sustainable free markets on the one hand, and limiting the power, role, and reach of the government on the other.

Greg Lindsay
Executive Director
The Centre for Independent Studies

INTRODUCTION

'Market Socialism' and China's Peaceful
Rise—The Case for Pessimism

Introduction
'Market Socialism' and China's Peaceful Rise—The Case for Pessimism

China is the fascination of our generation. It is the world's most populous nation and has sustained a high growth trajectory for almost three decades. Its rise is seen as perhaps the most significant illustration of economic transformation in history. From being perceived a little over a decade ago as a rogue power and one of the last, defiant bastions of communism in the world, China is now upheld as a new and compelling example of a successfully developing state. China's 'hard' and 'asymmetric' power is growing. Consequently, regional economic and security policies are overwhelmingly predicated on the 'inevitable rise of China', as if there were no other possibility.

Moreover, the recent Chinese experience and success suggests that there is no inextricable link between political liberalisation on the one hand, and the successful transition to a free market system on the other. Instead, the Chinese model seems to demonstrate that there are actually advantages to having a strong, authoritarian government heavily involved in the economy, overseeing the transition process and supervising the economy once transition is complete. Governments throughout Asia, Africa, South America, the Middle East, Russia and former Soviet Republics have all expressed various degrees of support and admiration for Beijing's approach, and there is no doubt that this 'Beijing Model' is furthering China's global influence. The magazine *Der Spiegel* recently asked in a major article: 'Does Communism work after all?'[1] For many, not only is the Chinese model passing the economic test, but it is fast establishing itself as an example of a successful and peaceful 'market-socialist dictatorship' on a historical scale.

Being optimistic about the future of China assumes that market socialism will be a successful system in transition. This book is about the sustainability and consequences of the *current*

Chinese political-economy model; and optimism or pessimism regarding this approach of 'market socialism'. Put simply, the case for optimism argues that the current approach can sustain China's economic and 'peaceful rise'. For some, China has managed to merge successful economics with authoritarian politics. At the very least, authoritarian political regimes can be useful in providing a degree of transitional and institutional stability in guiding a rapidly modernising society through the uncertainty of social and economic change. For others, China's brand of political authoritarianism is perhaps undesirable but not a serious economic impediment against future prosperity.

On the other hand the case for pessimism (which I make) argues that a politically unreformed China cannot sustain its economic and peaceful rise; that 'market socialism' is neither an example of a successful dictatorship or a system within which the transformative forces of 'market capitalism' have taken root; and significant political reform is unlikely to occur in time or in the forseeable future. Instead, the regime's pervasiveness, interference, and control over key areas of the economy, society, and institutions have led to frightening economic, political and social deficits—making China's current trajectory precarious rather than promising.

To be sure, there is no shortage of optimists, ranging from the cautious to the unbridled. In some cases, the reasons for, and extent of, optimism is unfounded but in many others, the case for optimism is both well thought out and formidable. Many optimists are sensible and distinguished scholars who have carefully watched the story of modern China unfold. Nevertheless, I argue that even the most sensible of optimists fail to present compelling evidence that the Chinese 'hybrid' authoritarian model can overcome its profound and mounting contradictions, tensions and dysfunctions. On the contrary, I argue that behind the high growth rates, the current Chinese approach of 'market socialism' is seriously flawed, failing and unsustainable. In this sense, the evidence is accumulating that the case for pessimism is the more compelling if not yet irresistible conclusion. Furthermore, significant political reform needed to limit the role of the Party and government faces formidable obstacles and will take some doing while the regime's determination and desperation to remain in power is potentially destabilising for the region. Consequently, China's successful 'peaceful rise' is both an untested and unreliable assumption.

Background—praise and optimism for 'market socialism'

In 2004, former World Editor of *Time* magazine Joshua Ramo, authored a paper arguing that China had become an alternative and successful model for developing countries, and that this model 'offered hope to the world'. Released by the influential The Foreign Policy Centre based in London, Ramo argued that the success of the 'great China experiment' had led to the rise of a so-called Beijing Consensus. The Beijing Consensus rejected 'big shock' and 'rapid liberalisation' reform and development strategies once favoured by Washington and other governments in the West. Instead, the Chinese model was a 'gradual', 'flexible' and 'ad hoc' reform model that emphasised pragmatism over doctrine. Unlike recent financial crises in Russia and Argentina, this had the advantage of fostering economic development without the destabilising effects of 'big shock' therapies. Moreover, such a 'flexible' model allowed countries to choose their own path towards development without political and institutional interference from the West. For Ramo, China offered the world a 'new physics of power and development'. Its model was the driving force behind the growth of Chinese 'asymmetric' power and influence in the world.

The gradualist approach of the Beijing Consensus has caught on. Since then, the optimistic case for the Beijing's pragmatic, hybrid model has been eloquently put by scholars such as Professor Meghnad Desai, Director of the Centre for Global Governance in London, and Albert Keidel from the Carnegie Endowment for International Peace. Both make a sensible case for why the Chinese model is sustainable. For example, Professor Desai argues that China is simply following elements of the successful growth strategies employed by Asian economies such as Japan and South Korea.[2] Its authoritarian politics is a Western obsession that does not deserve negative scrutiny. Keidel argues that China is good at 'capital' investment strategies that feed its 'growth' such as construction and infrastructure, and that the financial savings of its people guarantee that this strategy can be maintained for a long time. Further, China is well on its way to a well functioning open market even though there is some way to go. It has eased restrictions on the movement and deployment of its workforce and created a flexible domestic labour market that rewards hard-work, risk-taking and knowledge. In opening up its economy to global commerce it has enhanced its economic flexibility and financed new technologies and innovations. Like other successful Asian economies, the foundations for a thriving middle class have been laid—supported by land reforms, improvements in education and improved social safety nets. The soft institutions needed for markets to flourish are being built. Social order necessary for economic development is secure. The regime is showing encouraging signs that they are willing to tackle corruption within the country. Laws guaranteeing property rights have been passed. For Keidel, the Chinese Communist Party (CCP) overseeing this transition is proving to be a regime 'that is far more nimble and robust' than many presume. Although mistakes and miscalculations are made, the CCP is generally 'a confident leadership implementing a sophisticated and balanced policy' when it comes to government authority, social stability and continued reform.[3]

These arguments represent the case for sensible optimism fairly. They recognise China's progress and the enormous challenges that China must still overcome. No one can credibly argue that the Chinese model is out of the woods. But as a recent joint study by four leading scholars from the Center for Strategic and International Studies and the Institute for International Economics optimistically conclude:

> [I]t would be prudent for the United States to base its strategy on the assumption that China will continue to grow rapidly and become an ever more significant factor in the global economy. China faces many domestic economic challenges … But the strong likelihood is that China's leadership will undertake the further reforms necessary to meet its economic challenges.[4]

On the other hand, a handful of experts also mainly in the US, such as Minxin Pei from the Carnegie Endowment for International Peace and Gordon Chang, have cast doubts on the 'miracle' and the sustainability of China's rise in its current shape. Will Hutton in the UK has also recently proffered similar arguments. However, the overwhelming consensus in the US, Europe and Australia is one of general optimism.

'Market socialism' and the case for pessimism

The history of East and Southeast Asia shows that embracing open markets (and limiting the role of government in the economy as well as restraining its power) and unleashing its forces can lead to sustainable prosperity and fundamentally transform polities in the longer term. Much optimism is based on the belief that China has embraced the free market and this will transform the country into a stable, prosperous and vibrant one. China is yet another brilliant illustration of the marching of free markets toward prosperity, say these optimists. Its political system should be of secondary concern if it is relevant at all. Chinese politics might eventually liberalise—and perhaps it is inevitable given global market forces that have been unleashed in its society—but it will do so in its own good time. Meanwhile, we should encourage China to continue its current course. Countries such as Taiwan stand as a compelling model of what China might become sometime in the future.

We know that economic reform was explicitly undertaken to revive the legitimacy of the Chinese Communist Party (CCP) and re-orient and entrench its position and rule. Yet, the Chinese model treats free markets as selective and 'therapeutic' rather than 'transformative'. The 'Leninist corporatist' Chinese model as it stands denies that political authoritarianism must give way eventually as markets open. On the contrary, it assumes that a regime in the sole seat of power can successfully oversee a prosperous and thriving Chinese economy - despite retaining significant control over the economic resources and wealth of the country, and the most important sectors of the economy. In the words of Keidel, China's authoritarian political system can do the job of successful reform—the system is more nimble and robust than pessimists believe.

The first phase of reform which lasted until the mid-1980s was undoubtedly successful, as was the movement of labour from the country to the city. This largely involved the breakup of centralised communes in the 1980s, and the rural to urban migration in the early-1990s that was driven by the export boom. The reduction in poverty, which has been spectacular, was achieved overwhelmingly during this period. Importantly, these reforms did not threaten the existing structure of political power or interests. By the mid-1990s, however, the steam had run out of these reforms. Newer, more fundamental reforms were needed.

The second phase since then (from mid-1990s onwards) has been much more problematic because political power and interests are fundamentally affected. Behind the impressive growth figures, China is beset by serious problems in its banks, the structure of its economy, and the chronic mass misallocation and waste of capital to support inefficient state-controlled industries and sectors. The efficient and effective functioning of production and resource allocation is severely inhibited by an entrenched and systematic corruption which stems from single Party dominance and influence over the bureaucracy, and judicial, administrative and commercial organs of the state. Moreover, not only are these problems intertwined but they are the direct result of the regime's pervasive place, role and function within Chinese economy and society. Although China is frequently characterised as a free market economy, the state retains a significant role. About 56% of China's fixed assets are owned by the state. State owned corporations receive about 70% of capital even though they produce only about 30% of China's output. The problems in its economy essentially arise from the regime's hoarding, use and misuse of the country's resources—arising from the lack of restraint and limits on a regime that is not subject to the rule of law. The CCP's determination to retain power prevents the building of the soft institutions needed for successful capitalism: enforceable property rights, independent courts and rule of law, and independent financial and administrative organs. These would be 'transformative'—something the regime is working hard to prevent. Instead, its 'therapeutic' approach to free markets is failing. Moreover, problems are deepening and have been getting worse since the mid-1980s after the first stage of post-1978 reforms lost steam and the next and current stages were implemented. China's 'market socialism' is a far different animal from what we might call 'market capitalism'. Much of its apparent success is illusory.

China has come a long way and many believe that the regime will continue to meet its ongoing reform obligations. However, apparent virtues of the Beijing Consensus or Chinese model— gradualism and flexibility—are largely convenient strategies for an economically predatory regime to gain new footholds for hanging onto power; and initiating limited free-market reforms are new means to that same end. Moreover, while it is true that the Party is not fully in control of the transition as new forces and centres of power are unleashed, neither is the transition a runaway and irresistible force that will necessarily compel the Party to relinquish control. China has not yet reached the point of no return in which the power of free markets to transform has taken root. Indeed, recent history shows that the Party can still do much to hold-off necessary reforms that would significantly erode their reach and power. Importantly, the Peoples' Liberation Army (PLA)—still the most organised force within Chinese society and often forgotten in many analyses— remains sceptical of further liberalisation. We therefore need to seriously consider the possibility, if not probability, that reform will neither be profound or rapid enough to sustain China's spectacular growth

There are also further complications for China. As a result of the regime's politically expedient and economically predatory practices, substantial social and political deficits have been accumulating which strike at the heart of the Party's legitimacy and capacity to govern effectively. Behind the staged appearance of strength and unity by the senior leadership for the sake of international appearances, the CCP is an authoritarian regime that is increasingly seen as corrupt, desperate and ineffective within China. Unfortunately, this has caused the Party to become more determined and desperate to hold on to power - not less - no matter the cost to China or its people.

Although there are similarities, China's model is not the

successful model used by Taiwan, Japan, Korea or Singapore. Many optimistic viewpoints fall short due to inadequate consideration of China's political realities and the formidable political obstacles preventing further reforms that are needed during this transition. Genuine economic liberalisation— needed to propel China toward sustainable prosperity— would seriously threaten the Party's hold on, and ability to monopolise, power. The Party has maintained control of the most important levers of power in society despite three decades of reform. Although far from a monolithic entity, that the Party as a collective will easily roll over and voluntarily accept the economic logic of limiting their power, reach and influence is extremely unlikely.

We can present the question of China in another way. Market capitalism is an evolutionary process and successful instances of it do not conform to one static model. Adam Smith, Joseph Schumpeter, Peter Bauer and Friedrich Hayek have all made this point persuasively.[5] Does Chinese 'market socialism' represent an example of a successfully evolving capitalist system? I argue that it does not. Not all variations are healthy. Instead, China's 'market socialism' in its modern form is a predatory, dysfunctional and grossly inefficient system that is enormously wasteful and unsustainable. Unfortunately, it is perpetuated and deep-rooted as a result of political imperatives. I argue that 'market socialism' is not a successful example of capitalist evolution; there is no new 'physics of development' evolving and a strong dose of scepticism is needed as we watch China's modern development. Far from presenting an alternative conception or mounting a challenge, the dysfunction of China's 'market socialism' should be seen as doing much to affirm the enduring and connected logic of free markets, limited governments that operate under restraints and are subject to the 'rule of law', and sustainable prosperity.

Revisiting China's 'peaceful rise'

China's 'peaceful rise' is grounded in the proposition that China requires a stable and peaceful environment to develop its economy and modernise. Its embrace of global trade and foreign investment, as well as the settlement of outstanding border issues with Russia, Mongolia and India was a step in that direction. The argument that China needs peace in order to rise certainly seems a well grounded and reasonable one.

But the logic of a 'peaceful rise'—although a powerful one—competes with other forces within Chinese politics and society. As countries scramble to position themselves to benefit from China's self-proclaimed 'peaceful rise', relatively little attention in foreign and security policy circles is given to the combined consequences of a Chinese economy with deep structural problems, a Chinese society suffering profound governance and social deficits, a redoubtable army (PLA) that remains suspicious of the free market and the costs of embracing globalisation, and an increasingly desperate regime rapidly losing credibility with its own people.

How might domestic pressures influence foreign policy? Examining the frailties and flaws of the Beijing Consensus and Chinese political-economy model is a vital step towards answering this question. China is undertaking a tumultuous transition as the regime desperately hangs on to power. It should not be taken for granted that 'peaceful rise' logic will emerge triumphant over alternative possibilities.

What are the ramifications for regional security? I argue that the widely held belief that China will remain a stabilising influence in the region should at least be reviewed, since the interlocking segments for the 'peaceful rise' argument—that China will continue its impressive rise as an economic power, and that it will integrate seamlessly and peacefully into the regional and global status quo—remain at best a matter of speculation.

There are already worrying signals that should not be dismissed. Behind China's 'smile diplomacy', there are clear signs of a trend towards a 'chauvinistic nationalism' emerging within Chinese society, which has been both fuelled and exploited by a distressed regime in the name of national unity and dignity. The predominant driving force of an unsuccessful state or regime in transition might very well take a different and less predictable direction. In particular, the PLA remains a critical factor in the future direction of Chinese politics and society. The dynamics of transition with respect to relations between the CCP, PLA and segments of the population are ever evolving; and in the event of an unsettled transition, potentially troubling. This could increase the escalation possibilities of unresolved crises, particularly in the Taiwan Straits and the Diaoyu Islands.

More broadly, calls to either 'contain' or 'engage' China fail to capture the enormity of the challenge of 'getting China right'. While it is clearly beneficial and in the national interest of Australia, the US and its allies to primarily 'engage' China rather than 'contain' it in the Cold War sense of the term, the argument that mere engagement will lure China away from authoritarianism towards forms of greater democratisation is defective. The time has long passed when we could carefully 'manage' China's rise, when we could lead it willingly onto a liberal path. As Robert Kagan observes, 'The history of rising powers, and their attempted "management" by established powers, provides little reason for confidence or comfort.'[6] Remaining authoritarian is precisely what 'market socialism' implies. China's rulers do not intend to see a transition that will ultimately usher in greater political and economic freedoms, even though the current authoritarian set-up will be shown to be flawed, ineffective and duplicitous. It is clear that our capacity to influence domestic developments within China is severely limited. However, in 'engaging' China, we should not be blind to the implications of 'market socialism' nor simply accept that the Chinese model has been and will continue to be successful.

Finally, it is one thing to ardently hope, as Ramo does, that over a billion Chinese will achieve enduring prosperity in the coming decades. It is another to explicitly or tacitly support a political, economic and moral logic that is failing. The Chinese case study is a test case of whether authoritarian systems of heavy government participation and command in the economy can resist or even enhance the operation of free and open markets. Market systems evolve and do not conform to one definitive model. Is 'market socialism' an example of a successfully evolving capitalist system? I argue that it is not. Not all variations are healthy and sustainable. That modern-day China will inevitably follow the logic of a proven path towards prosperity (and be a force for stability in the region) rather than the path toward stagnation or turmoil should be debated rather than assumed.

Part A
CHAPTER ONE

The Rise of Chinese Power
and 'Market Socialism'

Chapter 1
The Rise of Chinese Power and 'Market Socialism

Introduction

Shortly before his passing in November 2006, Milton Friedman granted an interview to *The Wall Street Journal*. The transcript of the interview was printed in January 2007. During the interview, Dr Friedman was asked about whether he had any thoughts on the China versus India comparison. He replied:

> Yes. Note the contrast. China has maintained political and human collectivism while gradually freeing the economic market. This has so far been very successful but is heading for a clash, since economic freedom and political collectivism are not compatible. India maintained political democracy while running a collectivist economy. It is now unwinding the latter, which will strengthen freedom of all kinds, so in that respect it is in a better position than China.[1]

Most experts do not share this pessimism about the sustainability of China's current political-economy model. Instead, many are dazzled by the modern Chinese experience, and with good reason. Hundreds of millions have been lifted out of poverty since 1979. China's official growth rates have been hovering at, or close to, the double digit mark each year since 1978 when reforms began. The country's economic modernisation program is seen as one of the most spectacular illustrations of economic transformation in global history. Various projections from international organisations such as the OECD to the investment banking firm Goldman Sachs predict that China will overtake the US economy in terms of aggregate output (but not per capita output) sometime between 2020 and 2050. While recognising that the Chinese have a number of serious challenges to overcome in order to sustain these phenomenal growth rates, there is general optimism that these challenges can and will be met. Increasingly, based on the record to date, many are already prepared to declare the 'great Chinese experiment' a success. In contrast to Friedman, Greg Sheridan in *The Australian* has already declared the Chinese model an example of 'a successful dictatorship'.[2]

It is not surprising that developments in China are demanding global attention. China stands as a re-emerging colossus in the heart of Asia. While enormous resources and attention are presently directed towards the so-called 'War on Terror', long-sighted experts are more willing to bet that responding to a 'China growing strong'—the 'China question'—will be the defining question for the next few generations. The presumption that this century will be the 'Chinese century' is undoubtedly gaining momentum.

In Australia, despite a commonplace assumption that the China question is a recent phenomenon, the rise of China has been an anticipated and often feared event since the Menzies period. The sheer size of China makes developments within the country a matter of international significance. A country with about a fifth of the world's population and consistently high growth rates will always generate significant interest and excitement. Furthermore, when we consider that 'Red China' is now becoming more and more a hub of economic activity that is not just tied into, but increasingly driving, global economic growth, the 'China question' is one of the great questions for our age.

Economists put forward various scenarios for the future of China: positions that range from the wildly optimistic to the depressingly pessimistic. What all these positions do agree on is that China's future will depend on the continuation and success of its reform process. Any economic models used to predict China's future all necessarily make assumptions about the capacity of the Chinese economy to continually reform. As this deals with future activity, the continued rise of China is as uncertain as the possibility of its decline.

Milton Friedman argued that 'political collectivism'—in this case China's political authoritarianism and political statism—is incompatible with 'economic freedom', that is, the successful operation of a free market. Part A of this book argues that although the decline of China is far from inevitable, China's political authoritarian system—'market socialism'—is both a fundamental cause of existing problems and a significant barrier against further reforms needed to sustain China's rise.

This is not to say that authoritarian systems are always agents of economic decline. For example, Hong Kong and Singapore both boast thriving open economies. Although both are small 'city-states' which make comparisons with larger countries difficult, both nevertheless achieved their economic success within an authoritarian set-up. However, Hong Kong and Singapore share the commonality of limited government interference and predation in the economy. In China's case, I will argue that its deepest problems are caused by the role and reach of the regime at all levels of China's economy, society, and judicial and administrative organs. The key to China's future will therefore depend largely on limiting the regime's role and restraining the regime's power at all levels of the economy and society.

In this sense, restraint and accountability of the ruling regime within the country is essential. This is a political challenge. If political reform—in the form of greater embrace of political restraint and accountability—is not forthcoming, then the case for pessimism in terms of the future of China is strong. Yet, there are significant and entrenched obstacles to turning around the great ship that is the regime, or even changing its course. Keidel's depiction of the Chinese authoritarian system as nimble and robust is misplaced because China's authoritarian regime is at the heart of its problems. Although no one can predict the country's future, its current tensions and contradictions are profound, frightening and ultimately unsustainable. In other words, the current Chinese *political-economy* model and the country's trajectory is seriously flawed and in need of significant revision and reform.

The Beijing Consensus and the decline of 'democratic capitalism'

Joshua Ramo, the journalist who first coined the term Beijing Consensus, argues that:

> China is in the process of building the greatest asymmetric superpower the world has ever seen, a nation that relies less on traditional tools of power projection than any in history and leads instead by the electric power of its example and the bluff impact of size.[3]

Milton Osborne already calls China the 'paramount power' in the region.[4] At the heart of rising Chinese prestige and soft leadership is the emergence of China's alternative political economy model—the so-called Beijing Consensus—against various Western liberal archetype models. Before looking at the Beijing Consensus in greater detail, it will be useful to provide a brief setting of the historical and political landscape prior to its emergence.

During the Cold War, the Soviet Union and communism provided a seemingly coherent ideological alternative to economic and political liberalism. The collapse of the Soviet Union contributed in no small way to the perceived 'triumph' and universality of Western values and institutions, in particular the merging of liberal politics with liberal economics. It was what Michael Novak famously called 'democratic capitalism'.[5] Successful economics needed complementary 'soft institutions'. A democratic system and a liberal social ethic that encouraged pluralism and individual freedoms were not just seen as desirable but the adoption of them was assumed to be critical to guarantee the operation of free markets, entrench genuine meritocracies, ensure the spread and adoption of knowledge and more innovative processes, and restrain the predatory natures of ruling regimes and their tendency to use resources for self-serving purposes. Democratic institutions and free societies use and allocate resources more efficiently in the long run since the predatory practices of governments are restrained. A liberal democratisation process was therefore linked with successful developmental economics.

As the prospect of great power inter-state political and military conflict waned in the decade after the Cold War, the focus returned predominantly to economics. The Western and particularly American enthusiasm for rapid economic liberalisation as the strategy for developing countries was at its peak during this time. However, the record of developing economies that adopted rapid economic liberalisation measures since 1991 has been mixed. Chile was an example where rapid economic liberalisation seem to work. The Argentinian financial crisis between 1999–2002 was a noteworthy instance of where it did not. Even prior to this, questions were already being asked about the rigid and rapid implementation of wholesale 'neo-liberal' reform—so-called

Washington Consensus principles—in struggling economies. For example, the 'big shot' therapy (to rapidly privatise, liberalise and deregulate) administered to Russia following the fall of the Soviet Union had mixed reviews, while countries like Malaysia defied neo-liberal IMF prescriptions by restricting the free movement of their currency following the 1997 Asian Financial Crisis; a move which has been seen as largely successful. Rapid economic liberalisation as a 'fix all' for struggling economies became a blunt instrument of change. Insisting on it began to appear more doctrinaire than enlightened.

Nevertheless, 'capitalism' in some form or another still seemed the way forward—for example, from the more 'liberal' systems in Britain and America to the 'stakeholder' systems in Continental Europe. Market capitalism was evolutionary and everyone became entitled to their version of capitalism—it did not have to be a headlong rush towards implementing an American or Anglo-Saxon version of it. Capitalism in all its forms remains triumphant but it was the impetus for political liberalisation and democratisation that lost steam. As Timothy Garton Ash argued recently in *The Guardian*:

> What is the elephant in all our rooms? It is the global triumph of capitalism. Democracy is fiercely disputed. Freedom is under threat even in old-established democracies such as Britain. Western supremacy is on the skids. But everyone does capitalism. Americans and Europeans do it. Indians do it. Russian oligarchs and Saudi princes do it … Karl Marx would be turning in his grave.[6]

Ash makes an important point. Societies do not have to be 'democratic' or 'liberal' to 'do capitalism'. This was especially the case with transitional states. Almost 40 years ago, Samuel Huntington famously argued that the most effective way of dealing with the transitional stresses of rapid modernisation was to promote effective long-term political institutionalisation while maintaining strong, centralised authority. As he put it, in terms of development, the degree of government matters more than the form of government. Huntington even suggested that authoritarian regimes could provide a degree of transitional political stability necessary to guide a rapidly modernising society. However, Huntington's caveat regarding the advantage of authoritarian approaches must also be remembered in that the comparative advantage of strong, authoritarian government was short-lived and transitive in nature. In the longer term, political power had to be institutionalised to be effective and democratic institutions were superior in their capacity to adapt and respond to emergent pluralistic forces.[7]

In reality, any (causal) connection between economic and political liberalisation was taken for granted and rarely expounded by post-Cold War leaders in any compelling or comprehensive way. Correlation is not causation. The fact that the liberal-democratic West outlasted and outgrew the Soviet Union did not in itself establish a causal connection between political and economic liberalisation. Even at the height of Reagan's Cold War revival in the 1980s, Michael Novak had warned that:

> It [the relationship between economic and political/individual freedom] is too easily taken for granted because the habits of the heart are learned in childhood, supplying reasons that reason has forgotten.[8]

The West might have won the Cold War but there was not just one version of 'capitalism' on offer. It became unclear whether free market economics had to be allied with political liberalism, or whether political liberalism was necessarily the end game. Any link between political culture and economics became less clear.

Rise of the Beijing model of 'market socialism'

Crossing the river by feeling for the stones
Deng Xiaoping

Critics of 'liberal' and 'neo-liberal' approaches as well as 'democratic capitalism' might have gleefully pointed to instances where Western neo-liberal and liberal prescriptions failed to resurrect the economy but there were few successful counter-models on offer. The European Model gathered little speed outside the

Continent such that Martin Wolf was recently moved to ask in *The Financial Times*: 'Is the European model broken?'[9] The 'Asian values' and 'Asian way' debate in the 1990s, largely initiated by then Malaysian Prime Minister Mahathir and Singaporean Prime Minister Lee Kuan Yew, had lost much of its momentum after the 1997 Asian Financial Crisis. Besides, 'hybrid' countries like Singapore and Malaysia were not significant enough to present a fundamental challenge to Western ideas that after four decades of global struggle had earned a hard fought victory over those ideas of the Soviet Union and communism. Economies that successfully modernised were still mainly 'democratic capitalists' or at least headed that way. Western and American models favoured by the IMF and World Bank might have been problematic but there were few alternatives more appealing.

It is in this context that the so-called Beijing Consensus emerged as an alternative model for developing countries. As mentioned, the term Beijing Consensus was first used by a former journalist Joshua Cooper Ramo in a 2004 paper sympathetic to the Chinese reform experience since Deng Xiaoping in the late 1970s.[10] In the paper, Ramo argued that China had resisted implementing textbook IMF prescriptions, and this defiance of particularly 'big-shock' Washington Consensus principles had been proved successful. In reality, the Washington Consensus was a soft target since the 'consensus' (if one existed at all) had been increasingly discredited since the Argentinian crisis. Nevertheless, for Ramo, Beijing had introduced 'a new physics of development and power'. In rejecting destabalising 'big shock' neo-liberal therapy, the Chinese had developed a model that was flexible and gradual rather than radical. Importantly, the model allowed the Chinese (and presumably any followers of this model) to fit into the global system 'in a way that allows them to be truly independent [and] to protect their way of life.' Certainly, the latter characterisation tapped into an underlying current of suspicion and cynicism that buying into rapid neo-liberal reform was an agenda put forward by Western powers to shore up their influence and entrench American hegemony in particular. As Ramo argued:

> What is happening in China at the moment is not only a model for China, but has begun to remake the whole landscape of international development, economics,

society and, by extension, politics. While the US is pursuing unilateral policies designed to protect US interests, China is assembling the resources to eclipse the US in many essential areas of international affairs and constructing an environment that will make US hegemonic action more difficult.[11]

Although the Chinese leadership has never explicitly used the term Beijing Consensus, and there is no evidence that the Chinese Communist Party (CCP) initially set out to expound a model to explicitly compete with any 'consensus' about development, there is little doubt that an ever increasing number see Beijing's model—'market socialism'—as a competing development approach against Western archetypes, of which the increasingly discredited (and difficult to pinpoint) Washington Consensus was just one. Moreover, for the growing numbers of China optimists, the Beijing model is arguably the new 'exemplar' for developmental political-economy—the new example of how it should be done. Kishore Mahbubani argues that China's example is a better and more palatable example for Muslim countries such as Indonesia, Pakistan, and Bangladesh to replicate.[12] Commentators like Ramo argue that it is generally better to do what the Chinese are doing, which evidently works, than what the West and the Americans tell you to do, which may not.

However, unlike more rigid formulations such as the Washington Consensus, the Beijing model does not offer a set of coherent axioms that other economies can easily follow. This is perhaps the point of it and its attraction. The basis for much of its appeal is as a pragmatic and hybrid political-economy model. Models should be adapted to suit the existing political, social and economic conditions within that country—not the other way round. In this sense, the power and persuasion of the model really lies as much in what it rejects than in what it accepts.

First, by putting forward a 'gradualist' reform philosophy, the Beijing Consensus rejects the 'big shock' rapid reforms once favoured by Washington (and the largely discredited Washington Consensus). Reform does not have to mean large scale economic and social instability that 'big shock' therapies would cause. Reform programs can also be 'flexible'. Hence, since there are no pre-determined reform measures that *must* be accepted, nor are there timetables that *must* be followed, the Beijing Consensus provides backing for regimes that would otherwise incur the criticism of Western, neo-liberal reformers urging greater and more rapid changes. That in itself generates a considerable amount of prestige for China and enhances the legitimacy of the Chinese reform model.

Second, the Beijing Consensus denies that there is a necessary link or causal conection between successful economic development and political liberalisation. On the contrary, some supporters argue that authoritarianism had its advantages over the inconvenience and chaos of liberal-democracy, as the single-Party system has been an advantage in determining the pace of necessary reforms and pushing them through. This is the basis behind the 'successful dictatorship' that Greg Sheridan suggested China is becoming. In this context, one prominent commentator in Britain even went as far as to say that the alternative Chinese political-economy model is 'the biggest ideological threat the West has felt since the end of the Cold War.'[13] The refutation of 'democratic capitalism' is at the heart of the challenge the Beijing Consensus presents to long held liberal beliefs. As Sheridan argued in *The Australian*, 'China shows you can have [economic freedom] without [political freedom], where we used to think they were indivisable.'[14] Even prominent *New York Times* columnist Thomas Friedman has admitted that he has 'cast an envious eye on the authoritarian Chinese political system, where leaders can, and do, just order that problems be solved.'[15] Where once Washington (and perhaps Brussels) was seen to be the repository of developmental wisdom, such wisdom is now seen by many to be self-serving and even dangerous; eyes are instead transfixed on Beijing.

Third, this defiance of Western economic and political prescriptions as well as Western assumptions about 'democratic capitalism' is enormously prestigious for a China with growing regional and global leadership ambitions. The old logic—that democracy would follow economic liberalisation—had been a cornerstone of Western assumptions about the benefits of engaging China and 'managing' China's rise.[16] China's refusal to be managed by the West and reluctance to offer judgment against the policies of other states (its so-called 'live and let live' approach) is fast becoming an example and inspiration for developing countries and governments to follow. Governments in former Soviet Republics (like Kazakhstan, Uzbekistan and Turkmenistan), South America (like Argentina, Bolivia and Brazil), Asia (like India, Malaysia and Vietnam) and Russia have joined 'pariah' states such as Iran, Cuba, North Korea and Myanmar in publicly expressing a fascination and admiration for the Chinese political and economic approach. For example, Brazilian President Luiz Inácio Lula da Silva sent his advisors to Beijing to study 'Chinese economics' while declaring that the Chinese and Brazilian economies 'should serve as a paradigm for South-South cooperation.'[17] Singaporean Prime Minister Goh Chok Tong remarked that 'China's extraordinary development sets the standard for other Asian countries to follow.'[18] Muyingo Steuem, a senior Ugandan government advisor, told *The Financial Times* that 'In developing countries, China is regarded with a mixture of envy, admiration and awe.'[19] Meanwhile, the powerfully seductive rhetoric of a new Chinese exemplar that secures greater 'independence' of action (from the West and especially the US) as well as stability and prosperity is being put forward.

Why the rise of Beijing's model matters

It should be obvious that assessing the Beijing Consensus is clearly of enormous importance. Already, the argument can be made that countries like India and Russia are using the rhetoric of the Beijing Consensus as an excuse to drag their feet on promised reforms in the name of 'gradualism'. Developing countries in Asia, South America and Africa are looking to Beijing, and not Washington, for inspiration and guidance. Granted that 'big shock' approaches have had mixed results and are no longer recommended for profoundly undeveloped economies, but an approach that offers no criticism of tardy reform timetables seems a dangerous 'consensus'. Moreover, shallow reforms can easily be passed off as 'feeling for the stones' and finding one's own way when once they might have been perceived as policies designed to plaster over significant cracks.

Since the link between development and political liberalisation is severed, a new leader emerges, and a new legitimacy is established, for regimes that are indifferent towards, or hostile to, Western style liberalism. The rise of the Bush Doctrine as an extreme manifestation of liberalism (and the negative international response to it) was certainly not helpful to liberalism's cause. Nevertheless, from this perspective, the example of Beijing is pernicious and the potential danger and disruption to the Western-backed global liberal-democratisation project is enormous.

China is evidently not blind to this opportunity. China's political relations with regimes tinkering with illiberalism and authoritarianism through its 'rogue aid' and other policies is intended to win and influence illiberal friends (and in some cases secure natural resources for its development).[20] Its political and financial support offered to brutal, dictatorial regimes such as those in Myanmar, North Korea, Zimbabwe, and Iran (as well as other 'problematic' regimes such as those in Laos and Cambodia) for pragmatic, strategic and other reasons, disregards any global consensus about the value of democratic norms. China's authoritarian example and leadership—underpinned by the prestige of its political-economy model—comes only shortly after a time when winning the Cold War for many meant that the democratisation of the world seemed inevitable in the same way that free market economics won over its rival. The Beijing model challenges this perception that it is the 'end of history' and that great and small nations will simply roll over and accept the triumph of liberalism and democracy rather than challenge the establishment of the global liberal-democratic order, its norms and rules of engagement.

There is also a further related aspect to China's 'stubborn illiberalism' as far as the 'China security question' is concerned. Besides economic gain, Western economic and diplomatic engagement with China has twin motivations. First, following elements of liberal 'evolutionary-institutional' logic, it is hoped that as states further embrace the free market and 'buy into' the globalised neo-liberal system, they will be forced to eventually liberalise and ultimately democratise internally. Second, by entering the global marketplace, China will be forced to accept the current security status quo in Asia (with the US as the predominant power) because China needs a stable region in order to grow its economy. Peace would be China's overwhelming priority meaning that China would be loath to risk military confrontation with any power. This is certainly the reasoning China offers for its self-termed 'peaceful rise' or 'peaceful development', even as the Communist Party denies that the liberal 'evolutionary-institutional' logic *must* hold.

Australian Prime Minister John Howard evidently draws from the latter 'peaceful rise' perspective in terms of engagement with China.[21] For example, in the most recent DFAT *White Paper*, while recognising that 'China's rising economic, political and strategic weight is the most important factor shaping Asia's future',[22] the same document speaks mainly about building a 'strategic economic relationship with China similar to those Australia has established with Japan and Korea.'[23] Although there might be hiccups along the way, it is hoped that China will eventually be just another successful regional Asian partner bound by the peaceful logic and pragmatism of interdependence and economic ties. Incidentally, Opposition Leader Kevin Rudd, a fluent Mandarin speaker and former diplomat stationed in China uses a similar logic in putting forward his 'engagement of Asia' as one of three pillars guiding Labor Party foreign policy.[24]

Yet, important questions must be asked about these assumptions. Regional peace was a fundamental prerequisite for economic development for all the successful Asian economies. But contrary to Chinese intentions, Japan and South Korea eventually moved away from authoritarian traditions to become settled democracies in the region. Even elites in Singapore and Malaysia—successful economies with largely authoritarian systems—have been seriously wrestling with questions about walking the path towards further democratisation. Former American President Bill Clinton predicted in 2000 that 'We will be unleashing forces no totalitarian operation rooted in last century's industrial society can control' in lobbying for continued trade with China. President George W Bush repeated this logic in 2005, stating 'I believe a whiff of freedom in the marketplace will cause there to be more demand for democracy.'[25] While many simply believe that the 'evolutionary' process of liberalisation and democratisation will sooner or later catch up with China, the fact remains that the vast majority of political elites in China are determined and desperate not to let it. Does this matter?

'Market socialism' denies that liberalism and democracy is the end game for successful economies. It even denies that limited government involvement in, and command over, the economy (as in Singapore and Hong Kong) is a prerequisite for success. Chinese political and military elites are unlikely to simply roll over and accept this 'liberal evolutionary logic' as inevitable. Will pressure to democratise from within or without, particularly alongside internal economic, political and social pressures, prove volatile? The internal and external consequences of China's 'stubborn authoritarianism', as far as our security policy assumptions are concerned, are critical questions. Part B will consider some of these questions.

Assessing the test case

While China's rise provides challenges and opportunities that rightly concern and excite the world, its rise (or its decline) should not be taken as a *fait accompli*. No one knows what or where China will be in 10, 20, much less 50 years time. This book focuses on an assessment of the sustainability and success of China's current political-economy model, its likely trajectory, and the possible ramifications of this.

The 'Beijing model' *is* China's modern journey, and China is *the* test case for the approach. China's perceived successes up to now are the driving forces behind the momentum for the Beijing Consensus being seen as a new and improved model of economic development and political governance. It therefore stands to reason that if China's model were to falter, if its political-economy were shown to be profoundly flawed, much of the steam would be taken out of the Consensus. 'Market socialism' could not be seen as a successful example of capitalism's evolution. A central question in Part A therefore concerns the viability of China's authoritarian model as one capable of promoting sound and sustainable growth.

There are many studies on the success of and the challenges facing the modern Chinese model. The weakness of many of them lies in the absence of any method to assess the prospects of future success or failure—which really means the absence of argument about whether China *is able and willing* to meet its reform obligations and challenges. As stated above, it is important that such assessments be made as these questions have enormous implications for how we view developing economies, the relationship between economic and political reform, and what security policy challenges might await should present trends continue.

Part A
CHAPTER TWO

The Politics of Market Socialism

Chapter 2
The Politics of Market Socialism

Introduction

Despite the challenges faced by China being well known, the vast majority of China watchers are optimists. Pessimists are few and far between. For optimists, China's rise is the next exciting installment of Asia's economic rise since World War Two. The fact that China was the centre of communism in Asia, and remains so, make its rise even more intriguing and spectacular. The optimists speak about a remarkable transformation and strong prospects for the future; the pessimists about 'hype' and even 'mass delusion'.

Although recognising the vast challenges, many economists speak approvingly of the Chinese hybrid model, which is correctly seen as a pragmatic and flexible one. There is no a priori plan or pace to economic reform and no rigid conception about what the economy has to look like in the future. The fact that the Chinese model is a hybrid model is not a problem in itself; all economic systems are hybrids to some extent and there are multiple paths towards prosperity. However, many economists discussing the virtues of the Chinese hybrid model fail to consider and appreciate the politics behind 'market socialism'. This is a serious omission. The evidence in the following chapters shows that political imperatives define, restrict and drive the development and evolution of the Chinese economic model. The Chinese model is not simply an economic model but a model of political-economy. This is a crucial distinction. Statistics about growth rates tell a small part of the story. The Chinese model was largely developed as a strategy for political survival by the regime. Consequently, I argue that focusing on the politics behind China's model offers a fundamentally better understanding of what is occurring in China (and also China's future) than pure economic analyses and models can offer.

China's growth rates—The limits of linear quantitative analyses

China's rise has been spectacular, with growth rates between 7–10% every year, and the doubling of GDP every ten years since 1979. Can this be sustained? Using linear analyses to make predictions for the future is seductive but not always sound.[1]

Numbers alone should not drive the debate about China's future prospects. Why? For one decisive reason, many of the numbers we have are a product of guesswork, obfuscation, and in some instances, downright fabrication. For example, although most sceptics agree with Thomas Rawski, a University of Pittsburgh economist, that China's pre-1998 growth figures 'were in the ballpark, although it may have been a large ballpark', China's post-1998 growth figures remain doubtful.[2]

The circumstantial evidence suggesting recent significant inaccuracy is strong. While the world is dazzled by its ostentatious shows of wealth—the $365 milion Beijing National Theatre; the countless glass high-rises that adorn Shanghai; the $500 million Beijing Stadium that will be revealed in 2008—important pieces of information are inconsistent. For example, Rawski has pointed out that China's spectacular economic growth numbers in the late 1990s were in contrast to stagnating formal figures for energy consumption, freight transport and air passenger miles. In 1998, all but one of China's provinces reported GDP growth rates above the national average—an obvious statistical impossibility. China's National Bureau of Statistics (NBS) consistently revises figures received from the provinces downward yet refuses to disclose their methodology for doing so. While economists like Rawski present well documented calculations to suggest that total economic growth since 1998 has been about a third of the official figure, and generate significant media attention in doing so, NBS officials continue to vigorously defend the accuracy of their numbers without explaining how they arrive at them. Even one of China's domestic institutes, the China National Economic Research Centre, estimated that growth from 1978–98 averaged about one percentage point below official figures. Whether sceptics like Rawski are actually correct or not, the point is that the numbers we are given cannot presently be verified and conducting the debate using these numbers, as many economists do, is likely to pose more questions than answers.

Besides, even if we do accept the official numbers, it is still difficult to know how to view them. For example, Martin Wolf of *The Financial Times,* used data from economic historian Angus Maddison to show that up to 2004, China's much admired GDP per head (at purchasing power parity) rose by 370% at 6.1% a year during 1978–2003. Yet between 1950 and 1973, Japan's GDP per head had increased 460% at 8.2% a year. From 1962–1990, South Korea's GDP per head rose by 680% at 7.6% each year, while Taiwan's rose by 600% from 1958–1987 at 7.1% each year.

These figures suggest that China's official growth rates, while impressive, are not history making. As Wolf argues, 'What is remarkable is not how quickly China's economy has grown, but rather how slowly it has done so'[3] especially when we take into account China's low base to begin with.[4] They also serve to once again focus attention on China's model of development in which the politics behind the Chinese model needs to be examined. China's recent political story cannot simply be conflated with a broader East or Southeast Asian one.

Politics behind the Chinese model

> We have repeatedly declared that we shall adhere to Marxism and keep the socialist road. But by Marxism we mean Marxism that is integrated with Chinese conditions, and by socialism we mean a socialism that is tailored to Chinese conditions and has a specifically Chinese character.[5]
>
> *Deng Xiaoping*

The trajectory of China's history leading up to the reform period from 1978 onwards stands apart from much of Asia. For much of the twentieth century, China remained insular and suspicious of the West and Western institutions and ideology. While other now successful Asian states struggled at the time to develop their hybrid economic liberalisation and modernisation models, China persisted with schemes and programs designed to 'perfect' and define the agenda for communism in China with disastrous and tragic results.

Despite the trauma and barely imaginable cost in human life of the 'Great Leap Forward' and 'Cultural Revolution' in particular, Chinese leaders from Deng onwards emerged with an enhanced belief in statism (that is, significant state or ruling party intervention in social and economic matters). For example, the Cultural Revolution, which was officially condemned in 1981, has had a profound impact. It was seen as an irrational revolution fueled by 'popularism' and was a lesson against too much popular participation in government, not too little. The same lessons were drawn from Tiananmen in 1989; political elites believed that democracy would only lead to chaos. China has 31 provinces, over 650 cities, 48,000 districts, seven major dialects and about 80 spoken tongues. Only autocracy and monopoly rule could achieve order and keep China unified. Any political reform had to be kept in-house, that is, within the Party itself. As Deng argued:

> The purpose of reforming the system … is precisely to maintain and strengthen Party leadership and discipline, not to weaken or relax them. In a big country like ours, it is inconceivable that unity of thinking could be achieved among several hundred million people.[6]

The socialist command economy and grand initiatives like the Great Leap Forward had patently failed. Previous production methods had failed to offer China sufficient 'surplus value' that any modernising country craved and needed. However, even though the decision was taken to experiment with various market reforms, the political rationale driving it remained steadfast and unchanging. Economic reform was needed to revitalise the Chinese economy. Deng came to realise that this had to be complemented by political reforms in which excessive centralisation and bureaucraticism were seen as the greatest obstacles. However, as Minxin Pei from the Carnegie Endowment for International Peace argues, any political reform was restricted to administrative streamlining. Deng and his successors rejected institutional checks and balances that would have diluted CCP power.[7] Maintaining the continued political dominance of the CCP was the ultimate objective and not negotiable. This is the starting point for understanding the politics behind 'market socialism'.

There are two important political aspects behind 'market socialism' and the need for economic reform. Both relate to entrenching and continuing the legitimacy of CCP authoritarian rule.

First, when Deng introduced the beginning of the modernisation program in 1978, he was keen to emphasise the reinvigoration of socialism, not the death of it. Just as Mao distinguished Chinese from Soviet Communism by describing the former as 'communism with Chinese characteristics', Deng represented economic reform as 'capitalism with Chinese characteristics'. The reforms would be socialism's next stage of evolution. This was a deliberate and clever continuation of the Chinese *narrative* of socialist revolution redesigned and re-branded for the contemporary audience. To be sure, Deng could have hardly represented the reforms as an abandonment of socialism. This would not have been acceptable to the Party elites and would have undermined the basic legitimacy of the Party's existence and right to rule. Consequently, the foundational rhetoric of the socialist creed remained intact: keep the socialist road; uphold the dictatorship of the proletarian; uphold the leadership of the CCP; and uphold Marxist characteristics.[8]

Second, economic reform was a response to an emerging crisis of legitimacy for the CCP. Democratic regimes rely heavily on the ballot box to derive their legitimacy to rule. Authoritarian rulers who reject popular elections still require popular consent and legitimacy to survive and be effective. The charismatic leadership Mao provided either as executive ruler or figurehead could not be replicated. The flames of revolutionary fervour had cooled and (socialist) ideology mattered less and less. Put briefly, the circumstances that once propelled to power and entrenched the legitimacy and rule of the CCP no longer existed; a realisation devastatingly reaffirmed by Tiananmen in 1989. Given the economic need to reform in any event, Deng saw the role of the

CCP in driving ongoing reform as a renewal of the CCP's purpose. In other words, the legitimacy of the CCP to remain in power was now increasingly tied to delivering economic prosperity and growth rather than as the repository for, and leaders of, ideological revolution. Since 1978, the succession of leaders, from Deng to his appointed successor Jiang Zemin to current leader Hu have all sung from the same song sheet in terms of staking the CCP's legitimacy on China's ability to deliver consistent growth. Just as the CCP once delivered China from imperial capitalists, this new phase of history sees them leading the nation towards economic prosperity.

The political and economic success of earlier reform—A brief summary

Reform in the late 1970s and 1980s was largely a period where little political capital was spent or sacrificed. Chinese reform consisted mainly in the decentralisation of authority, decision making and resources. This was done almost completely within the context of the existing hierarchical structure. Local and regional authorities who were still CCP members and loyalists were given greater authority and responsibility to make decisions that were once ordained from the top down. The basic rules and exercise of property, capital and administration of power did not change a great deal, except that local economies were opened up for limited market-orientated and entrepreneurial activity under the stewardship of local authorities.

In terms of the rural economy, the most noteworthy and successful initiative occurred when large state-owned collectives gave way to the household responsibility system (HRS). Farmland, although still owned by the state, was reallocated to individual households by fix length contracts.[9] After fulfilling procurement quota obligations, farmers were allowed to sell surplus crops to an open market—usually country fairs. The government also reformed the pricing system and higher prices were set for state purchase of farm products. The HRS greatly improved the incentive structure of agricultural production. Farmers were given more autonomy in the production decision and allocated resources to more profitable activities such as orchards, fisheries and animal husbandry. Between 1978 and 1995, total factor productivity in agriculture almost doubled.[10] The success of the HRS was an early indication of the benefits of reversing decades of Mao's communism and limiting centralised control of production. In her book *How the Farmers Changed China*, Kate Zhou characterised the developments as a 'spontaneous, unorganised, leaderless, non-ideological, apolitical movement.'[11]

The emergence of Township and Village Enterprises (TVEs) was another happy accident of spontaneous, bottom-up activity. As farmers attained greater wealth, they experimented with non-farm enterprises and different forms of collective ownership. TVEs—a collusion between local officials and rural workers—generally performed more efficiently than older style state-owned-enterprises (SOEs) because the interests and actions of TVE managers and local leaders were more coordinated and mutually aligned. The property rights were still owned and controlled by Party members but these members were at the local level. Local leaders were provided incentives to help TVEs perform better and were discouraged from erecting roadblocks since the TVEs contributed directly to township budgets. TVEs proved to be spectacularly and unexpectedly successful. As Deng admitted, 'The result was not anything I or any of the other comrades had foreseen; it just came out of the blue.'[12] TVEs employed about 30 million people in 1979. In 1996, it reached a peak by providing employment for 135 million people (but has not increased since then). There is no doubt that rural economies would have been much worse had this not occurred. From 1978 to 1996, the rural workforce increased by 147 million. TVEs absorbed 107 million of these, usually at better wages than they would have received from working on farms.

More generally, the challenge of the initial phase (1979–mid 1980s) was to open the economy to trade and inward direct investment, and shift labour and resources away from agriculture towards manufacturing and services. The subsequent sectoral transformation of the labour force is probably the most dramatic manifestation of the reform process. The share of the labour force employed in agriculture has declined from 70% at the beginning of the reform period in 1978 to less than 50% today. China's shortage of arable land (about 15% of the land mass) meant that productivity in agriculture was always low. An OECD report estimated that productivity in the agricultural sector even today is about one-sixteenth the average in manufacturing and services when measured by output.[13] The result of this shift has been a much more efficient allocation of labour.

From the mid-1980s onwards, there was an increased focus on creating hard and soft market 'institutions' and 'processes'. In addition to intentions to reform or eliminate many of the notoriously inefficient SOEs, there was a need to foster the creation of a new dynamic private or 'entrepreneurial' sector to promote competition and innovation, and a greater reliance on market forces to inform key decisions such as commodity prices, capital allocation and wages. Prior to reform, bureaucrats in the State Planning Commission were responsible for allocating key assets such as steel and machinery. Nearly a quarter of all investment was financed through the state budget while the state heavily influenced the flow of bank loans which they termed 'policy lending'. The state also 'rationed' almost all conceivable consumer goods, and the State Price Commission set prices for most commodities and products meaning that there was little connection between price, profit and productivity. In the 1980s and 1990s, market forces increasingly displaced the planned decision making. In particular, market forces determined prices for most products, individuals were free to compete for jobs in a more flexible wage market, and rural or urban migration barriers were reduced.

The earlier phases of reform were undoubtedly successful. Importantly, since the existing political and social elites were generally protected and had their privileges preserved, there was little opposition to these earlier reforms from entrenched interests. The privileges of bureaucrats and workers in particular were largely untouched. The power of local Party officials actually increased as the system became more decentralised. Moreover, these earlier reforms led to immediate increases in output which helped to compensate the small numbers of losers during this period. In this sense, the authoritarian model was not really problematic for reform since embedded interests remained largely untouched and it is arguable that maintaining a decentralised, but still authoritarian system was in fact an advantage as decentralisation could be pushed through more efficiently while maintaining the existing political set up. Moreover, there is evidence that the success of the TVEs in particular actually increased much of the population's appetite for further reform.

One prominent expert on China's economy believes that about 80% of the 200 million people lifted out of 'poverty' since 1978 occurred in the 1980s.[14] The consensus within and outside China is that by the early 1990s, these initial reforms had run their course. A new shot of reform activity was needed. Yet, China's reform experience since the 1990s has been varied. I argue that China is now entering its most vulnerable stage. Economic, social and political imperatives have become increasingly contradictory rather than complementary.

'Gradualism' and emergence of the 'authoritarian trap'

'Gradualism' rather than 'big shock' is at the essence of the Chinese model. The intended strategy had been to 'grow out of the plan' meaning that the initial wave of reforms would give way to further changes that would make the Chinese economy more competitive.[15] One of the main aspects of 'growing out of the plan' was to encourage a significant non-state sector to flourish alongside the existing state controlled one. Many argue, with some merit, that it was a prudent strategy, considering the Russian experience in which there was an immediate loss of output following the dismantling of many state owned corporations in the rush to privatise. Moreover, it was mooted that the gradual decentralisation of decision making would move from the rural provinces, to the cities, and finally to state enterprises and other public bodies. Once local authorities and individuals became more practiced at making decisions for themselves, market initiative and enterprise would take hold and eventually flourish.

As we will see, 'growing out of the plan' has not been wholly successful. But there is a further political dimension and rationale behind gradually 'growing out of the plan'. 'Gradualism' also allows the authoritarian regime time and opportunity to co-opt the new winners and elites, placate those who possibly stand to lose their privileges, and in doing so retain authority as China changes. One of the few outspoken China pessimists, Minxin Pei, argues that:

> [T]he process of selective withdrawal creates strong incentives for the ruling elites to defend their last strongholds of economic and political privileges [while] gradualism allows the ruling elites to co-opt new social elites and form an exclusionary network that divides the opposition, while creating an incentive structure that rewards cooperation with the anti-reform elements and penalises opposition to such elements.[16]

Pei makes a good point that applies to almost all authoritarian systems trying to change and undergo reform. Gradualism is widely seen as a pragmatic and innovative strategy. What is less spoken about is the relationship between the strategy of 'gradualism' and what one might call the 'reform dilemma' faced by authoritarian political elites. As argued earlier, the CCP is determined to remain in power. This is a political imperative for almost all authoritarian regimes, and no less for the CCP. To do so political elites need to secure internal order and obedience. What they fear is the emergence of new elites within their own society that might challenge their political authority—a distinct possibility as fundamental reform is initiated and China's economic structure changes. This is the basis of the reform dilemma for the CCP.

As reforms continue, there are new winners, and existing winners who might stand to lose a great deal. To placate potential new losers and co-opt emerging winners, economic success is essential. Why? New winners from the reform process are the emerging middle and entrepreneurial classes in China. As a group, they can be expected to remain loyal or at least indifferent to the political status quo while they prosper in the new China. Tellingly, former President Jiang Zemin was forced to extend membership of the CCP to owners of private businesses in 2001 despite the protestations of some old-style hardline members.[17]

Those who stand to lose are those who benefited most from the old state run system: in particular bureaucrats and SOE workers. Economic success is more likely to lead the new rich to accept the legitimacy of authoritarian rule as there would seem no reason to rock the boat in such an era of prosperity. Economic success is also needed by the authoritarian regime to placate those who stand to lose, either by redistributing resources to soften the blow of reforms to disenfranchised groups, or indeed to buy off opponents or at least build coalitions with some of those groups. In this sense, economic success has become a source of legitimacy for especially authoritarian regimes of and in itself.

Where do reform dilemmas and authoritarian traps come in? On the one hand, authoritarian elites have an interest in economic success and progress. But on the other, they need to ensure that their exclusive political authority survives. To this end, and because they have the power to do so, authoritarian elites tend to establish systems that favour their own interests and those of their supporters. They tend to establish or perpetuate closed markets that the state or their supporters draw succour from. They also tend to shape financial policies that distort genuine open market activity to further their political ends. And finally, they tend to use the fruits of economic success to entrench their own positions.

In other words, even though the existence of the state is essential for order and economic growth, the state remains omnipresent and pervasive in economic activity and risks becoming a powerful agent of artificial economic decline. Authoritarian regimes that depend on economic progress for their survival, at the same time perpetuate conditions that threaten sustained economic progress. Pitting their right to rule based on economic progress is therefore a precarious (but necessary) activity for the CCP.

The emergence of the 'household responsibility system' in particular demonstrated the benefits of removing centralised interference and intervention. Optimists and pessimists agree that China faces enormous challenges. But the optimists argue that China can 'out-grow' its problems via an ever expanding economy. However, these optimists fail to appreciate the political nature of these problems and fail to present compelling arguments why the CCP can overcome this authoritarian trap. Commentators generally only see China's high growth rates and readily predict that China is well on its way to meeting its challenges. As I will argue, the evidence does not convincingly support the conclusion that the authoritarian trap can be overcome. What is needed to set China on a sustainable course demands less Party control and use of China's wealth and resources—policies that the CCP cannot accept as it attempts to remain in power. Growth rates in themselves tell us only a small fragment of the economic and political story, and peering behind them reveals a country that is much more dysfunctional and in more serious trouble than is generally admitted.

Critical areas needing further reform

The challenges that China must manage are increasingly well documented. Unlike the situation even just a decade ago, a lot more data is available and commentators have used them to offer a clearer picture as to what is happening within its vast territories. There is no need to go too much into depth here as these challenges are well summarised elsewhere.[18]

There are, however, clear development or economic 'fault lines' that will likely prove decisive. One cannot adequately discuss these challenges without fundamental reference to the politics behind it. They are, worryingly, areas where the authoritarian trap is most evident, where the most insidious forms of corruption reside, where the contradictions between economic, political and social imperatives are most apparent, and where the leadership has most notably and doggedly implemented their 'gradualism' strategy. To wit, they are areas where the flaws in the Chinese *political-economy* model are most evident. These are below and will be discussed in the subsequent chapters:

—reform of SOEs and key sectors of the economy;
—reform of the banking system; and
—reform of the system of capital allocation and use.

Part A
CHAPTER THREE

The Chinese 'Economic Miracle'—
What Lies Beneath

Chapter 3
The Chinese 'Economic Miracle'—
What Lies Beneath

Introduction

What sustains optimism about China's current model? First, its record of growth that has lifted hundreds of millions out of poverty is a compelling phenomenon. Second, those waiting for a Chinese meltdown have been waiting since 1978. There is a natural attrition rate for pessimism. Third, reform is well underway (although how far it has come does not in itself answer how far it will keep going). Fourth, the Chinese leadership and the official news agencies are consistently making the right comments that especially please Western observers. The Chinese have become masterful in the art of earnest diagnosis of their problems—a point of difference with most authoritarian regimes that remain in constant denial. (Unfortunately, the solutions proposed frequently differ from the action actually taken.) Finally, momentum from growing optimism can in itself fuel a measure of success. The more optimism there is, the more benefit of the doubt is given to a regime's ability to find solutions. In effect, more time is bought, and a more generous interpretation of developments is possible than would otherwise be the case.

It is worth looking at what lies beneath the 'Chinese economic miracle'. Some optimists underestimate the *extent* of China's economic and structural problems. Importantly, many others fail to appreciate that politics is at the heart of it. The primary economic strategy is growth. China will grow its way out of its problems. Yet, growth is not the ultimate objective—regime preservation is—and any pro-growth policy has to be understood alongside the constraints of these political objectives. Growth enhances the Party's legitimacy which in turn enhances its chances of survival.

However, the political objectives and constraints directly hinder the capacity of the regime to meet their contemporary reform obligations. These economic and structural problems should not be treated as separate and distinct. They are not only interconnected but largely result from China's 'market socialism'. Inefficiency, waste, misallocation and the pilfering of resources is at its most profound and widespread in areas where the political stakes are the highest for the regime; and consequently in areas where the regime is most involved. The regime's desperate attempt to hold on to power presents a formidable obstacle to further fundamental economic reform and sustainability.

Beijing's model of institutional corruption: a framework for pessimism

> I do not see a clear linkage between corruption and one-Party rule in China.[1]
>
> *Former Premier Zhu Rongji*

Former Premier Zhu is wrong. The most insidious, costly and destabilising forms of corruption in China have everything to do with the one Party system. In many respects, focusing on corruption draws together many of the reasons why the Chinese model is failing. 'Corruption' can simply mean public officials engaging in illegal activity for private gain. But it can also be the result of a clash of contradictory structures. Legitimate behaviour within a communist-authoritarian political system might very well constitute 'corruption' in a free market economic system. 'Systemic' or structural corruption is therefore frequently a problem for countries and societies in transition.

China rates poorly on all the global corruption rankings.[2] Commentators frequently cite President Hu's 'speak softly but carry a big stick' adage as firm evidence of the leadership's determination to crack down on corruption. This crackdown is seen as part of President Hu's aim to promote a 'harmonious society'. Fighting corruption is an important part of the strategy. Official Chinese news agencies are more than willing to report on the very public anti-corruption drives, and in particular the spate of high profile prosecutions and sackings (and even executions in some instances). These began in 1995 with former Politiburo member Chen Xitong, and in recent times have included the deputy Commander of China's navy, Vice-Admiral Wang Shouye, and Deputy Mayor of Beijing, Liu Zhihua, who was overseeing the city's makeover for the Olympics. The dismissal of Shanghai's Communist Party Secretary, Chen Liangyu, in September 2006 was another high profile catch.

Prosecuting corrupt individuals is laudable. However greedy individuals lining their pockets are a small part of the problem. The source of the most serious, debilitating and entrenched corruption stems from the relationship between the CCP on one hand, and the bureaucratic, economic, financial and judicial organs of the state on the other. The problems arise from the fundamental contradiction between a political party determined to maintain an authoritarian state (and retain control of significant resources within the country as well as judicial organs in order to do so) while introducing and benefiting from a free market economic system. Without an arms length relationship between political priorities, processes and functions on the one hand, and economic and legal ones on the other, free market logic is easily obscured. The system is denied the soft institutions required for the effective operation of an efficient market. This entrenched corruption can be portrayed in several ways.

First, free markets need independent courts to enforce rules and regulations, and to uphold contracts and payments. In China, granting and *enforcing* widespread property rights would strip away the power of CCP officials who essentially rule through the extraction of collective rents and poorly compensated seizures. Yet, enforceable property rights are intrinsic to any free market. But constitutional laws passed in 2004 that deem property rights as 'inviolable' and reflected in the much heralded property law passed in March 2007 do little to change the status quo. In commenting on these laws, *The Economist* observes:

> This latest law will not bring the full property-rights revolution China's development demands. Indeed, it will not meet the most crying need: to give peasants marketable ownership rights to the land they farm. If they could sell their land, tens of millions of underemployed farmers might find productive work. Those who stay on the farm could acquire bigger land holdings and use them more efficiently. Nor will the new law let peasants use

their land as security on which they could borrow and invest to boost productivity. Nor, even now, will they be free from the threat of expropriation, another disincentive to investment. Much good land has already been grabbed, and the new law will merely protect the grabbers' gains.[3]

Even in the case of non agricultural or land assets such as a 'private enterprise', it remains unclear who really owns what: whether it is really owned by the individual, local government or party unit. However symbolic the property law might appear, it does not alter the primacy of state ownership. All land still technically belongs to the state and urbanites can buy or sell properties only under long term leases (50 to 70 years). Moreover, any legislation, even if it were comprehensive and well crafted, cannot be relied upon while judicial officers are appointed and sustained by Party officials. As *The Economist* further observes:

> Should an underdog try to use the new law to enforce his rights, the corrupt and pliant judiciary would usually ensure he was wasting his time. Since the Cultural Revolution, when the NPC passed just one law between 1967 and 1976, the legislature has been legislating quite prolifically. But the passage of laws is not the rule of law.[4]

Second, the natural consequences of economic activity must be allowed to play out. Instead, political interference in economic processes is widespread. For example, in October 2001, the People's Supreme Court (China's highest judicial tribunal) ordered provincial courts to halt bankruptcy proceedings involving state enterprises. The central government had no problem with this being a legitimate decision within a 'free market with Chinese characteristics'. However, as economist Simon Pritchard commented, 'Capitalism without bankruptcy is like Christianity without Hell.'[5] The process of 'creative destruction' must be allowed to take place in any healthy system. More generally, rule of law necessary for private economic activity cannot exist adequately in China while the Party effectively remains the final arbiter in the legal system.

More generally, as mentioned, 'anti-corruption drives' are mainly focused on catching out 'corrupt' individuals. While the attention is firmly on the prosecution of high profile individuals on the take, there is certainly something questionable about the sincerity of campaigns to eliminate China's 'rampant' corruption (in the words of President Hu) when relationships inimical to the effective operation of free markets between political and economic arms are relied upon (or at least encouraged) by the one-party regime to maintain their system of patronage and reward that which is essential to remain in power. For example, 'free market' activity such as 'privatisation' simply affords greater opportunities for politically connected insiders to benefit. An estimated 30% of owners of privatised SOEs are CCP party members. In a recent study done by the regime's own researchers at the State Council, the Academy of Social Sciences and the Communist Party's central university, of the 3,220 Chinese citizens with a personal wealth of 100 million yuan (US$13 million) or more, 2,932 are children of high-level cadres. Of the senior positions in the five industrial sectors—finance, foreign trade, land development, large-scale engineering and securities—85–90% are held by children of high-level Party officials.[6] The reluctance to further open up SOEs, especially those operating in the most important sectors, to genuine competition and international standards of transparency is not politically viable. The Chinese authoritarian political-economy model relies on forms of entrenched corruption rampant in its economic system, is functionalised by proclaiming it official policy, and is needed to maintain their authority through the use of massive state resources to fulfil political objectives. The economic cost of this entrenched corruption, therefore, is much larger than various estimates that treat 'corruption' as a discrete problem and focus only on individual acts of greed, illegal quotas and levies between provinces and so on. Moreover, because political and much of economic life begins and ends with the CCP, the protection of rights is ultimately derived from political power or political connections. This entrenches corrupt activity with the CCP at its core.

Third, the successful logic of free markets also insists that capital must follow the tail of profit. The responsibility of allocating the majority of the country's investment resources cannot fall in the hands of a clique of Party members and their cohorts since no small grouping can ever have adequate knowledge of where resources are needed and how they are most efficiently and profitably deployed in such a vast country. Neither can so much of the country's resources be allocated for political rather than economic purposes without mounting cost. Indeed, the corruption of a system allowing the political control and use of so much of China's resources is really the concise summary of reasons for problems with the banks, SOEs, the allocation of capital and the lack of transparency of organisations. These economic 'fault lines' will be looked at below.

The banking crisis

Let's begin with the 'banking crisis'—there is really no other term for it. It is what Chinese economic expert, Nicholas Lardy, calls China's great 'Achilles heel'.[7] The financial assets of banks constitute about 98% of China's financial assets. The banking sector is dominated by China's Big Four state owned banks (SOEs by definition) which control around 70% of total bank assets. Other 'Policy banks' under direct control of the State Council control about 10% of assets while other urban and rural cooperatives control about 18% of assets. Private domestic and foreign banks therefore constitute a tiny minority (about 2%) of the Chinese banking sector.[8] China's banks provide about 80% of funding for all Chinese businesses. What happens to these state controlled entities therefore overwhelmingly determines the financial health of the country.

(a) Chinese banks and non-performing loans

A 2004 report in *The Economist* declared:

> If money circulates around a sound economy the way blood circulates around a healthy body, then outwardly robust China has a black hole for a heart. It is in the financial system that the contradictions in Deng's 'socialist market economy' are most apparent, with a banking sector that has built up a mountain of NPLs by lavishing cash on value-destroying state firms while starving deserving private borrowers.[9]

China's main banks have been technically insolvent for over a decade although they enjoy high levels of liquidity due to the high savings ratio of the population. The overriding problem is bad loans, and in particular non-performing loans (NPLs), combined with dwindling profits and accumulating losses.

Official Chinese figures consistently and significantly differ from those offered by reputable international commercial and research organisations. The former carefully conceal the methodology and data used to derive their figures. Chinese banks, according to international accounting firm Ernst & Young, suffer from 'a banking culture that resists openness and accountability.'[10] The latter openly cited the methodology and data they use. Chinese authorities are evidently feeling the pressure to downplay their problems.

As recently as 2006, Ernst & Young estimated NPLs of the Big Four banks to be US$358 billion and total NPLs in the financial system at US$911 billion.[11] This equals 40% of GDP. As a comparison, at the end of 2005, India's NPLs amounted to about 5% of GDP; Indonesia's was under 5%; and Japan's was under 3%. The report incensed the regime which demanded that Ernst & Young 'apologise' to China and immediately withdraw it.[12] The official Chinese NPL figure for the Big Four banks was only about US$150 billion. The Ernst & Young figure was comparable to figures produced by Fitch Ratings[13] and Standard & Poor[14] which were around the US$320–330 billion range.

These discrepancies between internal and external figures are not new. According to official Chinese estimates, NPLs amounted to about 9% of GDP between 1997 and 1999, which was considerable but not disastrous.[15] For example, Japan in the mid-1990s had similar NPL figures. However, even then, estimates by independent and commercial experts had put the figure at somewhere between 40–70% of GDP, with Standard and Poor, the most pessimistic of them, having cited the 60–70% figure.[16] A 2004 report by Deutsche Bank put the independent consensus estimate at about 40% and diplomatically mentioned that the differences could be down to the 'subjectivity of the evaluators'.[17]

Furthermore, before 2002, the standard used to judge a 'bad' or 'non-performing' loan was much more lenient in the Chinese system compared to international standards. For example, Chinese banks frequently just 'roll over' what Western institutions would consider NPLs so that they do not appear on the balance sheets as NPLs. Even if we accepted the official Chinese figure, a report by *The Economist* estimated that were the international Western standard of NPLs to be used, the NPL figure would be at least twice as high immediately.[18] Even after the international classification standard was adopted, official NPL figures remain the same instead of doubling as experts expected.

The estimates only reveal a small part about the extent of the NPL problem and various attempts at a cover-up. NPLs negatively affect the liquidity ratios of banks. To meet prudent financial standards and improve the overall appearance of financial health, Chinese authorities have used two techniques to improve these liquidity ratios, both of which are shallow tactical initiatives that only temporarily plaster over cracks.

The first tactic has been to simply use the country's substantial reserves (accumulated from the savings of its people) to periodically issue massive bail-outs by injecting money into the banks to grant them immediate relief. For example, in 2003, US$45 billion was injected into two of the Big Four state-owned banks alone. In 2005, the government injected about US$15 billion into one of the Big Four to push their capital adequacy ratio to an acceptable 8%.

The second tactic has been to transfer NPLs to recently created 'Asset Management Companies' (AMCs), hence removing these NPLs from the banks' balance sheets. In 1999, the Peoples' Bank of China announced that they unloaded about US$170 billion of NPLs to four AMCs as part of a grand recapitalisation plan. At the end of 2005, Ernst & Young estimated that US$330 billion of NPLs had been transferred from the Big Four banks to AMCs.[19] The theory was that AMCs would specialise in the recovery of debt, ensuring that the proportion of NPLs recovered would be significantly higher than if the NPLs had remain with the banks.[20] In return, the AMCs issued promissory notes and bonds to the banks for 50% to as much as 100% of book value. Using this strategy, Chinese officials widely reported that they expected to recover at least 40–50% of the NPLs.

Ernst & Young conservatively estimates the average cash recovery rate to be about 25%. The most generous recovery rates for these were estimated to be about 30% by Fitch Ratings, meaning a loss of 70%—significantly worse than the 40–50% recovery rate officials reported as the minimum. A Deutsche Bank report revealed that in 2003, the AMCs were burdened with about 19% of the state banks' NPLs and had liquidated about a quarter of these NPLs. The cash recovery rate was only about 20%.[21] Since promissory notes and bonds issued to banks are usually between 50–100% of the NPL book value, this strategy has simply created another class of financial organisation that has taken on the problems of the banks and will itself be laden with debt.

The use of bail-outs, especially using AMCs, to absorb NPLs has been substantial. The 2006 Ernst & Young report believed that in addition to the US$170 billion transferred to AMCs in 1999, from 2000–2005, the banks transferred an additional US$160 billion to the AMCs and wrote off US$157 billion of NPLs against current earnings. Of the US$330 billion transferred to AMCs up to the end of 2005, the AMCs have disposed of only about US$100 billion meaning that US$230 billion remain on its books. Additionally, there is about US$323 billion worth of NPLs elsewhere in the financial system, for example, in a so-called 'fifth AMC', Huida Asset Management Company, established in 2005, as well as in other state-owned investment companies and rural credit cooperatives.

Although official Chinese figures put the NPLs of the Big Four banks, after these transfers and write-offs, at US$133 billion at the end of 2005, this figure is significantly at odds with independent research by international banks and accounting firms. According to a research report by UBS, quoted in the Ernst & Young report, aggressive lending from 2002–2004 has resulted in a new wave of unreported NPLs that could be as high as US$225 billion. Ernst & Young estimate that over the past 15 years, the Big Four banks alone have created about US$845 billion in bad loans (which includes this UBS estimate of US$225 billion from 2002–2004.) Even after all the NPL transfers and write-offs, the Big Four banks have about US$358 billion of NPLs on their books, which is more than double the official estimates.

The Ernst & Young bottom line, which it describes as 'conservative', is that there is US$358 billion worth of NPLs in the Big Four banks, US$230 billion in AMCs and US$323 billion elsewhere in the Chinese financial system. This adds up to an outstanding NPL figure of US$911 billion at the end of 2005; not too far below China's much heralded foreign exchange reserves of about US$1.07 trillion at the end of 2006. Bear in mind that in 2002, the corresponding Ernst & Young report had placed the entire NPL figure at US$480 billion.

To put in context what these numbers mean for the various banks, Fitch Ratings took individual bank figures, which excluded the liabilities of AMCs, and did an analysis on the figures for these banks. Taking the estimates for 17 of China's largest commercial and policy banks, they found that estimated losses swamped reserves and made a considerable dent in capital. For five banks, capital would be entirely wiped out.[22]

(b) Why bail-outs don't work

Back in 1997, estimations were that the bad loan ratio was rising at about 2% each year.[23] The increase in NPLs would be considerable since total loans by state owned banks doubled from 1995–2000. At the end of 1999, official figures indicated that 25% of all loans by state commercial banks were 'overdue'. Following a massive bail-out in 2000 when US$36 billion was injected directly into the banks and US$190 billion were transferred to AMCs, the Peoples' Bank was forced to admit that the percentage of NPLs in 2001 even after this bail-out was about 26%. In other words, as one notable China sceptic, Gordon Chang, observes, 'the biggest bank recapitalisation in China's history had no apparent effect on the health of its banks.'[24] Something is clearly askew with official Chinese figures. The various rescue tactics are also evidently not working.

That these tactical bail-outs were unsuccessful—in that NPLs began to pile up again shortly after each instance—is not surprising. Bail-outs in the form of capital injections merely restore the balance sheet to a healthier state. However if the proportion of NPLs (to performing loans) continues to increase, and the amount of monies loaned continues to increase, it is merely like a parent paying back a child's credit card debt while the child continues to spend more than they earn. The credit card company might be happy for a month while the minimum repayment is back on track but future grief is certain. Therefore, statements by many observers after each of these bail-outs that China's banks were 'back on track' misses the point.

Moreover, transferring the NPLs to AMCs might temporarily improve the balance sheets of the banks but it is not a long-term solution. The justification for transferring NPLs to AMCs was that AMCs would be in a better position to produce a better financial recovery rate from the NPLs.[25] Even so, as ratings agency Moody's stated at the time, disposing of NPLs will mean substantial book losses and 'the most important challenge for state banks in the next few years will be to increase quality earnings sufficiently to cover potential losses from NPL reduction.'[26] Given the disparity between the promissory notes and bonds issued by AMCs to banks to take charge of these NPLs, and the actual cash recovery rates which are significantly lower than the value of the promissory notes and bonds offered to the banks, the deal is a bad one for the AMCs in particular. More generally, all that occurs is the creation of new entities (AMCs) that are burdened with NPLs. Loans ultimately have to either be repaid or written off. Whether a bank or an AMC does this is hardly the point—the health of the financial system has not been improved by these circumventive measures.

(c) NPLs are growing

State-owned banks continue to *increase* loan monies even though the ratio of NPLs is actually rising. Loans have increased about 50% year on year from 2001 to 2004 according to Institute for International Economics (IIE) figures. Recent CEIC data shows that China's bank loans have increased proportionately with increases in deposit growth.[27] Total loans by local banks have reached about 145% of GDP while the IIE estimates that NPLs are now over US$535 billion (about 27% of GDP). Deutsche Bank estimates that it could be as high as US$830 billion.[28] Bear in mind that these figures do not include NPLs that have been written off (following the bail-outs) or transferred to AMCs.

In a normal market economy, you would limit the practice and introduce severe standards for loan approvals. In the unique Chinese 'market socialism' system, banks are forced to continue to issue loans according to non-market principles. The Party had, from the very beginning of the reform period, decided to retain authority over the financial sector. State banks have the primary function of supporting government policies, and the secondary function of acting as financial intermediaries in a market economy. The 1994 *Commercial Bank Law* states that after a transition period of 'unspecified duration', all banks are to operate as independent entities. Meanwhile, they must lend according to economic, social and political needs as specified by the State Council. This includes, most notably, financial support of insolvent or struggling SOEs (despite these SOEs operating in generally highly protected sectors). Indeed, about 75% of NPLs are loans to SOEs and collective enterprises. The free flow of 'policy lending' has led to the observation that China is the only country in history to have achieved both record economic growth and record numbers of non-performing bank loans simultaneously.[29]

Mass capital misallocation

Although some optimists readily acknowledge the extent of the problems within the Chinese banking system, experts like Fan Gang from the National Economic Research Institute in Beijing argue that financial risks are manageable given the high growth rates of the economy. Growth will not only secure the continued legitimacy of the Party, Fan argues that China's economic growth will be the panacea for its debt burdened banks.[30]

This reasoning depends on faulty logic. It completely bypasses why—in the desperate pursuit of growth—so many loans fail to perform in the first place. Instead, it carelessly assumes that high growth rates necessarily indicate a healthy economy and that China can outgrow all its political and economic problems. The reality is that massive amounts of capital are being wasted on firms that have little incentive to use this capital efficiently or responsibly.

According to a recent IMF study, 75% of China's growth comes from capital accumulation.[31] In other words, growth is largely the result of pouring money into investment projects. Fixed asset investment increased by over 25% in 2005. In the first half of 2006, it jumped a further 30%. Investment bank Morgan Stanley estimated that fixed asset investment probably exceeded US$1.3 trillion in 2006.[32] The state (through state-owned banks) directed over half of this and still owns about 56% of fixed capital stock. This would be an acceptable strategy provided that capital is used efficiently and productively. Unfortunately, this is not the case.

The evidence for the limits of this approach is strong. World Bank findings indicated that about one third of recent investments made were wasted.[33] In the 1980s and 1990s it took $2–$3 of new investment to produce $1 of additional growth. Studies from the last several years show that it now takes over $4 to produce $1 of additional growth. Recent Morgan Stanley and McKinsey & Co reports suggested that it was more like $5 invested for $1 of additional growth.[34] In other words, Chinese investment is getting less and less bang for its buck. Why is it taking more and more money to achieve the same level of growth?

China is suffering the effects of massive and chronic 'overinvestment', over-capacity and declining productivity. *The Economist* estimated that while nine out of ten manufactured goods were in oversupply in 2004, investment in fixed assets grew by 30% over the same period and contributed 47% of GDP.[35] In other words, increasingly large amounts of money are being poured into the production of goods that are not consumed or needed by the economy. This is reflected in the average levels of slow moving inventory in Chinese firms which are estimated to take around 350–360 days to sell and the levels of unsaleable inventory which are possibly the highest in the world.[36] This is a symptom of overinvestment and produces growth figures that are bulked up by 'assets' that will never be consumed.

In light of these trends, we would expect investment growth to decline as rationalisation takes place. Instead, the opposite has happened. According to Peoples' Bank of China data, capital investment from 2000–2005 doubled and bank investment loans increased by almost 10% in 2005. In the first six months of 2006, they increased almost 10.5%.[37] More and more money is being invested even as returns are diminishing.

Where is the capital going? General estimates are that China's SOEs consume over 70% of capital but produce less than 30% of output. This is despite the fact that the number of SOEs has more than halved from two decades ago. Government officials frequently pressure banks to support local expansion programs and politically expedient ventures with little regard to the venture's competitive advantage or economies of scale. As one report suggests, the relationship between banks and especially local officials (who are effectively the masters of the local branch of the bank) would be unacceptable in most market systems:

> Local officials have enormous leverage over the banks, because they administratively supervise the local branches of the state banks, they negotiate with the central bank over the amount of loan quota the local banks can lend, they decide how much of the existing loans to the local SOEs are to be repaid, and they are in a position to assist the banks in such matters as hiring, housing, and education of bank employees' children.[38]

The upshot is that capital allocation (in the form of credit) has frequently little to do with rational economic decision making. Banks effectively are fulfilling the fiscal priorities of the government through their 'policy lending' function: to reduce unemployment that would result from genuine rationalisation of SOEs and the industries they operate in, to foster social stability, and to continue support for workers brought up with an 'iron rice bowl' mentality of state support and employment. All this furthers the end of maintaining loyalty to the ruling Party.

In this situation, that capital is not put to good use is hardly surprising. Where once subsidies and grants from the central government's budget kept SOEs going during the Mao era, banks now effectively fulfil this fiscal function and are forced to lend heavily to SOEs to meet the CCP's political and social stabalisation goals.[39] A conservatively estimated 40% of bank loans to SOEs are extended on a 'policy' rather than 'commercial' basis while most loans to SOEs are afforded artificially low interest rates.[40] An estimated two-thirds of NPLs were given on a 'policy' basis. To argue that China can solve its NPL problem by rapidly growing is indeed blind logic.

The inefficiency of these SOEs (and other collective enterprises) is predominantly behind the waste and the explosion in NPLs. Peering into the murky workings of them presents a picture of enormous decay that places China's 'spectacular growth' in a darker light.

China's SOEs: When productivity and profits don't matter

Recent official figures by the World Bank, using official Chinese statistics, report that the return on equity by SOEs have increased from 2% in 1998 to a respectable 12.7% in 2005.[41] However, these are certainly inflated. The massive government 'subsidies' are included in this profit figure, 'investment income' (dividend distributions) is counted twice in the profit sheets, while gross profit margins have been declining steadily since 2005, mainly because of over-capacity.

In reality, the profitability of SOEs has been in dramatic decline since 1978. For instance, their profits per unit of gross output dropped from 15.5% in 1978 to 1.6% in 1997, while profit per unit of capital dropped from 22.9% in 1978 to 0.8% in the same period.[42] Predictably, many SOEs actually incur losses and the trend is worsening: with 19% losing money in 1978, 40% of them doing so in 1997, and 51% of them doing so in 2006.[43] This is despite the fact that about 150,000 of the roughly 300,000 SOEs have been closed or merged since 1978, which included many of the poorer performing ones. Whereas their losses totalled US$4.2 billion in 1978, in 1997 it was reportedly US$74.4 billion which meant total losses actually exceeded total earnings.[44] (Given the enormous amounts of capital injected into state banks to cover for NPLs that were lent largely to SOEs, the US$74.4 billion figure seems low.) In a recent report released by the IMF, and authored by World Bank China Director David Dollar and IMF Assistant Director Shang-Jin Wei, a survey of 12,400 firms in 120 cities in China was taken for the period

2002–2004. The study found that despite a quarter century of reforms, capital use by state-owned firms produced returns that were 11–54% lower than returns from capital use by domestic private and foreign owned firms.[45]

(a) Why are SOEs performing poorly?

Easy credit at low interest rates (set by the government) is one reason. There is little incentive to use capital efficiently since there is little pressure to justify the borrowings on commercial grounds, or to pay it back on time or at all. The CCP simply cannot allow too many SOEs to fail. A ready supply of capital is therefore used to offer subsidies or grants, or to ramp up production irrespective of whether the commodity is in demand or can command sufficiently high prices to achieve a profit.

A second reason is weak or ineffective management. SOEs are at the centre of the CCP's extensive patronage system that helps entrench the Party in power. According to extensive research done by Minxin Pei, the CCP appoints four in every five SOE managers and Chief Executives, and 56% of all enterprise managers. Even in 'restructured' large and medium sized SOEs that were transformed into shareholding companies, the Board Chairman was a Party Secretary in 50% of cases.[46] In the over 6,200 large and medium sized SOEs classified as 'restructured' in 2001, Party committee members of the pre-restructured firms became the board of directors in 70% of the restructured firms. Finally, about 8% of the Party's 70 million card carrying members, and almost 16% of urban members of the CCP, held executive positions in SOEs in 2003.[47] From these figures, it is clear that any reform or restructuring does not mean greater independence from the Party. Indeed, positions in 'restructured' SOEs are offered as reward for Party loyalty. In this light, SOEs backed by 'iron rice bowl' cultures and politically motivated Boards and management are more concerned about patronage and keeping employees on the books than productivity and profit. The continued prevalence of 'policy borrowing' and 'political spending' of capital should be expected.

Third, because SOEs are not run like normal commercial entities in a transparent manner, managers frequently do not actually know, or lie about, how the organisation is performing. For example, in 2003 the State-Owned Assets Supervision and Administration Commission was established to oversee SOE management. Newly appointed Chairman Li Rongrong announced encouraging profits for China's top 500 SOEs, reporting revenues of US$526 billion in 2003 (up 25% from the previous year) and profits of US$43 billion (up 33% from the previous year). According to Li, only 87 of the top 500 SOEs were making losses.[48] A year earlier, as Minister in charge of the State Economic and Trade Commission, Li announced to the CCP's 16th National Congress that since 1989, SOE profits had soared from US$9.5 billion to US$31 billion from 1989 to 2002.[49]

If that were the case, there is no plausible explanation for why so many loans lent to these same SOEs were effectively written off or passed off as NPLs, and why there was any need to transfer 1.4 trillion yuan worth of bad loans to AMCs in 1999. The point is that the official Chinese version of performance during this period is at odds with most credible and independent studies backed by empirical and numerical detective work. For example, even China optimists like Stephen Green from Chatham House acknowledge that the top 500 firms did badly in 2001 and profits year-by-year fell 37% in the first six months of 2002.[50] A study by Gary Jefferson and others suggested that the productivity of un-restructured SOEs declined 2.9% a year from 1993 to 1996 while productivity for 'restructured' SOEs (that became shareholding firms) performed even worse—declining nearly 8% a year during the same period.[51] The guesswork or dishonesty of reporting officials from economic ministries and bodies indicates a dangerous culture of reporting unreality, and reported figures are very often designed to appease or flatter rather than as the precursor to rational planning.

Fourth, the problem of a fragmenting market is a serious problem. Most blame the decentralisation initiatives of Deng's reforms which encouraged two developments. Local protectionism (for example, administrative barriers to trade and investment under the stewardship of local CCP leaders protecting their turf) flourished. Moreover, a form of 'fiscal feudalism' took root where local authorities were allowed to directly pocket taxes from the earnings of local SOEs. In 1979, local governments were responsible for 48.9% of public expenditure while the central government oversaw the other 51.1%. In 2004, the central government controlled 27.7% of spending while local governments assumed 72.3% of the fiscal role.[52] Decentralisation therefore encouraged the establishment of de facto economic kingdoms supported by local courts that are placed under pressure by local Party leaders to administer the law in a way that favours local firms (or ignores enforcing judgments made against local firms by other jurisdictions). One of the most high profile instances of this was an investigation into local authorities from the Heilongjiang Province who issued specific instructions to the courts to not enforce unfavourable judgments against 67 firms that appeared to be losing their cases.[53]

The point about fragmentation is that its contribution to overinvestment and economic waste is significant. The result is general duplication of production and capital use, increased local protectionism and inefficient local trade wars, and the distortion of product and factor (that is, 'factors' used in production such as labour and capital) markets. Rationalisation of production and economies of scale are simply less feasible.

From the outside, fragmentation might seem to produce good outcomes since raw output is increased.[54] Since the emphasis has been on growth, and more particularly, increasing output, the incentive to 'produce' is high. SOEs would rather produce inefficiently or continue to utilise only a part of their capacity than condemn themselves to closure.[55] Whether individual SOEs survive or are closed down has been assessed not so much on productivity or profit but on output. Given that SOEs were the backbone of the 'iron rice bowl' for workers, there is a strong social and political incentive for local authorities to ensure local SOEs survive to provide continued employment. They are therefore encouraged to do whatever is needed to be done—the result being the rise in local forms of protectionism, many of which are illegal.

Since the emphasis is on maximising local output, the distortion of both product and factor markets is undeniable. In product markets, to help absorb local production, local authorities erect barriers to entry for non-local products such as quotas, regulatory hurdles and fees. This 'autarchic' mindset is also much of the reason for excessive product diversification. In factor markets, local authorities frequently force local firms to favour hiring local residents, while obstacles are erected for 'foreign' workers in the form of fees and the need for permits. In capital markets, local authorities frequently interfere with the outflow of capital and restrict the investment and acquisition of local SOEs by non-local ones. Pei cites two examples of this. The first is the regulations in eighteen provinces that ban the sale of alcohol produced in other provinces. The second is the use of fees to protect local manufacturers whereby purchases of cars made in other provinces have to pay additional costs for registration and inspection. In 1998, the total of these protective levies was 160 billion yuan (while the whole automobile industry only made four billion yuan in profits in that whole year).[56]

The difficulty of fixing contradictions

> Basically all the tasks [needed to sustained economic growth] have been completed over the past four years. So I think this government has made good on its promises.[57]

> *Former Premier Zhu Rongji*

Optimism about the Beijing model's prospects is fuelled by the fact that the solutions are actually quite simple and well articulated, especially by Beijing. How do you fix the banks? Improve lending procedures and risk assessment policies, and find innovative ways of recapitalising them so that they can begin from a blank sheet with solid capital adequacy ratios. How do you improve the profitability of SOEs? Make them more responsive to the market by fostering competition and improving their corporate governance. How do you combat corruption and resource wastage at local levels? Make officials more accountable to the central government for monies spent and allocated and continue to come down hard on corrupt individuals. Further, make sure your judicial bodies are independent from governmental interference.

These universally accepted solutions are continually proposed by the investment banks and organisations like the OECD that offer status reports and updates about Chinese intentions to implement these measures and the small steps that have been taken.[58] However, these findings about what China 'must' or 'should' do miss the point and ignore the problem. There is little value talking about how adopting proven free-market economic principles (existing within a 'rule of law' system and an accountable executive) would fix the problem because China is not a normal 'free market' political-economy. For example, notwithstanding the OECD's tendency to do so, how seriously can we take the statement by Chinese authorities, including the Chairman of the China Securities Regulatory Commission, that they regard the OECD Principles on Corporate Governance as the international benchmark and are determined to meet it?[59] The debate is not about what China ought to do to fix their problems, for that is obvious, but whether China *can* or *will* implement these measures in time or at all.

(a) Political impracticalities: Fixing the banks and SOEs

There are several ways to genuinely improve the banking crisis, none of which are politically feasible for the regime.

The first is to simply stop lending to loss-making SOEs. This is the crux of the problem. Even if innovative ways of re-capitalising can be found—whether this is through AMCs, other forms of bail-outs, debt market bonds, increased securitisation and so on—the problem of insolvency will always return if bad loans continue. However, introducing better risk assessment procedures, training and hiring more risk assessors, and the whole range of international best practice standards will not do the trick. The problem is not a technical but a political one. The government is well aware that a large slice of loans will never be repaid, but for political reasons, it is forced to continue 'policy lending'. Even though one estimate is that SOEs are operating at a loss of 1% of GDP each year, they employ over one million soldiers and officers in the Chinese reserve military forces.[60] Cutting off these 'policy loans' would cause too many of the SOEs to fail (many of which are balance-sheet insolvent and kept operational only because they are 'liquid') and lead to even greater unemployment and loss of support for the regime.

Optimists cite statistics that suggest a fundamental restructuring of the economy away from SOEs. The number of SOEs was halved over the past decade while the proportion of employees working in

SOEs has declined from 19% in 1978 to 9% in 2003.[61] However, when you consider that 75 million workers were employed by SOEs in 1978 but still 69 million workers in 2004, the restructuring is not as wholesale as it might first appear.[62] Besides, the fact that a 'declining' number of SOEs (many have simply been merged together) are consuming an increasing proportion and amount of the country's capital is the bottom line problem.

Second, the state owned banks could be genuinely privatised meaning that monies raised from securitisation could be used to partially rescue the balance sheet. More importantly, management would be independent to make commercially plausible decisions on loans. Despite being cautiously optimistic about the future banking system, Jonathan Anderson, Chief Economist for Asia at UBS, is nevertheless forced to conclude that 'the fundamental problems (for Chinese banks) will not be fully resolved until the state gets out of the business of running banks.'[63] This, however, is unlikely to occur because the regime is not prepared to give up using the banks as an effective fiscal stimulus to support SOEs, and to create and sustain jobs through this spending. Over two thirds of all investment spending in China is initiated by the government and offered to state owned firms,[64] largely through the banks and to a lesser extent through the central budget (most of which is distributed to local channels). Over 60% of deposits are made into the four state owned banks alone and it is not conceivable that the CCP would give up its access to the bulk of resources used to prop up support for its rule. Allowing foreign corporations to own minority stakes in these banks—capped at 25%—will not do the trick. It is likely that this restriction will remain even as China fulfils other WTO obligations. Similarly, other 'solutions' that would release monies to be allocated according to market principles will be resisted. These include encouraging the rapid growth of independent banks to increasingly crowd out failing state-owned ones, a much larger corporate bond debt market, and allowing a genuine stock exchange to flourish where stocks in listed companies are freely and fully floated, rather than being manipulated by the government as the majority shareholder.

Third, there is a clear need to force SOEs to operate in more competitive, free-market environments where protection from private domestic and outside competition is relaxed, credit is not available at reduced rates and on 'policy grounds', and poor performance is punished (by falling profits) rather than rewarded (by further bail-outs.)

Finally, despite periodically adopting more and more international standards on corporate governance, while non-arms length relationships remain between state owned bodies, the regime, and the judicial, oversight and administrative organs, corporate governance and transparency cannot be effective. Professor Lu Tong who is a Director at the Chinese Academy of Social Sciences might even be successful in convincing us that there is indeed a Chinese tradition that stresses:

> A gentle man likes property, but he must have a moral way to get it. Corporate governance starts from a system and ends with honesty.[65]

Such sayings do not amount to much when the basic separation of relevant power and state organs required for greater governance and openness is lacking as a result of authoritarian imperatives. Why else would the regime seek to suppress any debate about official facts and figures, let alone official truths?

(b) China's failing record of reform

Recent figures tell a revealing and disturbing story about the pace and adequacy of reforms.

The regime is pinning its hopes and continued legitimacy on *growth*. The theory is that growth will create more jobs, allow SOEs to grow their way out of trouble (in terms of producing more to repay loans and become dominant producers in their sectors), and decrease the number of NPLs for banks (since SOEs will be able to repay more of the loans). The targets they have set in 2010 and beyond are almost all growth targets.

Lets take stock of the situation. How has the regime achieved this? It has been achieved largely with various forms of actual and de facto fiscal stimulus, namely through the budget but particularly through lending by the banks to SOEs. For example, according to official figures, fiscal stimulus alone contributed 2% GDP growth in 1999, 1.7% in 2000 and 1.8% in 2001.[66] Monies used for fiscal stimulus have increased from US$89.4 billion in 2002 to US$119 billion in 2005, an increase of over 33% over the period.[67] Moreover, monies loaned by China's banks have increased about 16% year-on-year since 2000 increasing at an annual rate of about US$150 billion in 1998–2001, to US$240 billion in 2002, to US$380 billion in 2003.[68] In the first half of 2006 alone, US$267.5 billion has been issued. Furthermore, an increasing proportion of sources of funds in the Chinese domestic financial markets are bank loans, rising from 72.8% in 2000 to 85.2% in 2003.[69] In other words, other forms of finance (such as corporate bonds and security finance which are 1% and 3.9% of domestic finance respectively) remain undeveloped and as the regime controls the vast majority of banking assets, the regime controls an overwhelming and ever increasing majority of credit in the country.

The government effectively directs about 70% of investment spending. What are the massive amounts of government directed money to stimulate growth being spent on? It is being directed mainly to SOEs (who receive about 70% of the monies) and spent largely on fixed asset investment where spending has been growing at between 20-30% year-on-year since 2000.[70] Capital investment as a share of GDP is now approaching and will soon exceed 50%, at about US$1.3 trillion, up from about 38% in 1999. At least half of this is initiated by government policy.[71] Unsurprisingly, according to 2003 figures which are the latest figures available, the state owns 56% of China's fixed industrial assets.[72]

Taiwan, for example, which had an unparalleled growth rate of 8% each year over 50 years never had capital investment spending of more than 30% of GDP.[73] China's figure is extremely high by any standards. Furthermore, fixed asset or capital investment growth ratios are way above that for GDP, about 4 or 5 to 1. This is behind the problems of overinvestment and overproduction that I have discussed. Even the Bank of China has criticised the 'blind expansion of seriously low quality, duplicate projects.'[74]

If this is occurring and is even acknowledged by the Bank of China, we would rationally expect something to change. For example, we would expect government credit and funds to be directed away from inefficient SOEs operating in the industrial sectors jam-packed with unused and unsalable inventory. In fact, the production of industrial products (one of the worse categories in oversupply) as a composition of GDP has remained almost constant since 1980 at between 44–45% of GDP.[75] In other words, SOEs keep receiving more money to make more products that cannot be sold or consumed. As these SOEs keep receiving easy and cheap credit, keep on producing wasted products and keep on defaulting on loans, it is no wonder the NPL ratio increases by about 2% each year. During the bank loan bonanza period of 2001–2003 where outstanding bank loans jumped from US$150 billion to US$380 billion, the latest research shows that about 40% of the increase in loans became nonperforming. After this disastrous result the authorities only lowered lending levels to about US$330 billion in 2004 which was then raised again leading up to 2005.[76] While SOEs use about 70% of total investment money, they contribute to about 30% of GDP. Given the regime's need to continually stimulate the economy for political ends, it is no wonder loans keep on increasing at record pace despite economic rationality demanding that it should not.

The disturbing conclusion is that despite a decade of knowledge about these problems and talk about reform and potential, the problems are getting worse, not better. The authorities are simply becoming adept at plastering over severe cracks. For example, the leadership was proud to announce that NPLs had declined from 25% to 21% as a share of GDP between 2002 and 2003. The progress is illusory since the decline was merely a result of the massive new loans issued during that time. As these new loans take time to become classified as nonperforming, NPL ratios temporarily improve. As NPL trends are increasing, the NPL figure will worsen. Shorter-term tactical measures will not overcome the contradictions within the model.

The limits of growth by stimulus—not just another Asian success story

China's rise is often simply treated as the next exciting instalment of an economic miracle in Asia, albeit one on a historical scale. To be sure, China has looked to Asia (especially Singapore) rather than America or Europe to guide its growth model. Some therefore argue that China is simply following the Asian model of growth.[77] Commentators, they argue, sceptical about China's rise would do well to look at the other economic success stories in Asia.

Indeed there are some parallels between Chinese growth and the Asian successes after World War II. Between 1950 and 1980, Japan grew at an average real rate of nearly 8%. From 1960–95, the Hong Kong economy grew at an annualised real pace of 7.7%, South Korea grew at 8.1%, Singapore at 8.4% and Taiwan at a stunning 8.6%. In Southeast Asia, 'quasi-tigers' like Thailand and Malaysia were not far behind. China's growth rates, accepting official figures, are similar to Asia's best performers.

Moreover, China currently shares another similarity with Asian high-performers, namely growth based on extremely high rates of capital investment, significant protection of domestic firms, and access to cheap and plentiful labour. This 'perspiration, not inspiration' strategy, as Paul Krugman famously put it, largely created growth as a result of capital inputs drawn from high domestic savings.[78] Productivity was never a large part of the Asian success equation in the earlier years.[79]

Even back in 1994, Paul Krugman warned that growth achieved simply through ever increasing 'inputs' (that is, directing enormous amounts of capital toward fixed capital investment) would yield diminishing returns.[80] In response, optimists might reply that there are two 'get out of jail' cards that the Chinese can use. The first is the so-called 'tiger in the cage' scenario: the world-beating saving habits of the Chinese. The idea is that the 'tiger' (savings in banks) once released will lead to a tide of consumer spending which will take up any slack from reduction in fiscal stimulus and also increase demand to help over-supply problems.

The problems with this position are threefold. First, savings are at such high levels largely because there are very few and poor provisions for social welfare, health and old age. Only about one-seventh of the population, for example, is covered by basic health insurance, so many households save to cover medical expenses. Families save for retirement because the basic pension scheme covers only about 16% of the economically active population— and in any case provides a pension equal to just 20% of average wages. Households also save for education. Primary school fees are a large financial burden, particularly for poorer rural households. It is unlikely that rises in domestic consumption will provide a way out.

Second, the average disposable income of urban dwellers is about US$1350 annually, growing at between 10–20% each year. In rural areas, it is about a third of that figure. It will be a long while before the US$5000 figure is reached, where discretionary spending is said to take off.

Third, the regime needs these savings in the bank because the banks need them to maintain liquidity ratios. The government simply cannot afford for there to be massive withdrawals from the banks to fund consumption led growth.

The other 'get out of jail' card is that Chinese SOEs can become increasingly innovative and learn to make better use of capital. For example, predictions about hundreds of thousands of recent engineering graduates flooding the economy and what it will do for innovation are commonplace. The problem with this scenario is that while SOEs—which receive the lion's share of capital—remain coddled and protected, there is no incentive to innovate. Moreover, too much capital is being denied to the private sector which is much more likely to invest in innovation, or invest innovatively. In other words, capital that should be reserved for innovators in the private sector is instead increasingly wasted on inefficient state owned ones whose productivity is about half that of private industry both by aggregate and sector.[81] Whereas in 1985–1990 the private sector accounted for 20.7% of all fixed asset investment, in 1996–2000 it was only 13.9%.[82] Clearly the SOEs consumption of a greater and greater proportion of the country's available capital is crowding out the private sector. During the past decade, there has been little evidence of SOEs changing their mindsets and taking this innovation route. Even China's most profitable three or four SOEs are far short of world class standards in terms of sustained innovation, performance and financials. Moreover, the capital lost to the private sector which really is the cradle of innovation is not measurable but surely significant. As highly regarded MIT economist Huang Yasheng argues:

> It is amazing how little attention the most important matters receive in the media, such as domestic entrepreneurship ... The main problem is that it does not have a fair, level playing field for domestic private firms while the big state-owned enterprises maintain

their lock on influence and access to capital … I am not an economic nationalist at all [but] it is really paramount that the country maximises the use of domestic entrepreneurial resources and talents. The key difference between China's reforms and those elsewhere since the Soviet Union collapsed is that the goal in the other transitional economies has been to institute capitalism, whereas in China the goal has been to preserve socialism.[83]

Finally, with respect to comparing models, even though China gained inspiration from the so-called Asian model of growth (investment in capital, emphasis on exports, and exploitation of cheap and plentiful labour and so on) the differences between China's model and those of successful East Asian economies such as Japan and South Korea are significant.

Huang Yasheng's insight that China's goal has been to preserve socialism rather than institute capitalism per se is important. Other Asian economies adopted the free market as a *transformative* strategy; China adopted it merely as a *therapeutic* strategy to preserve the regime's hold on power. While these other Asian economies encouraged and supported private enterprise and innovation, China is politically bound to direct the majority of its capital to prop up SOEs. The commercial and operational rights of foreign firms are given more protection than private domestic ones. Indeed, protection in over two dozen key industries that SOEs operate in (such as telecommunications, infrastructure, banking, construction) is primarily directed against private domestic firms from challenging SOEs. Combined with the lack of access to capital afforded to these domestic private firms, it is no wonder that China cannot produce any world class private domestic firms in key sectors of its economy. Even the state sanctioned Academy of Social Sciences was forced to admit:

> Because of long-standing prejudices and mistaken beliefs, private and individual enterprises have a lower political status and are discriminated against in numerous policies and regulations.[84]

Moreover, these other Asian models understood the importance of property rights, 'rule of law' and independent courts, independent bureaucracies and administrative organs, and the like. The regime in China, determined to maintain its power, control and relevance, is unwilling to allow these institutions to take root. Stock markets in China are generally used to raise capital (to keep SOEs afloat) and increase the share price for those firms with state backing (in which only about one third of shares are floated and the state retains majority ownership). It does not serve as an effective capital raising medium for enterprising private firms for which listing is restricted. There are only about 40 private firms of the over 1500 listed firms.[85] State bureaucrats are given powers to control the allocation of stock parcels (many of which go to CCP members) rather than allowing the market to decide. Ultimately, Japan and South Korea were prepared to embrace a free market political-economy: accept a limited government philosophy in all major aspects of the economy and society, embrace 'rule of law' systems to restrain governments and its agents, and more generally allow the transformative effects of these markets to take root. The Chinese regime is not. Despite the fact that China has looked to other countries in Asia for inspiration, one should be careful about drawing too close a comparison between their various models.

Hazards for the regime

Even the most flawed and inefficient systems can survive for years beyond all expectations. Although no one can predict an imminent economic crisis or its timing with certainty, there are several trigger variables to watch out for.[86] The key to the CCP maintaining power is co-opting new elites and appeasing newly created losers. To do so, the Party has to prolong its control of and access to resources, which means continued access to the enormous savings pool. Tax revenues are a less efficient and feasible option to access funds, given the fragmented (that is, decentralised) and non-transparent nature of China's economy. Access to bank savings is much more valuable.

There are still few options outside depositing savings in state owned banks and buying government bonds. The regime has been successful so far in stifling financial diversification. The great threat, therefore, comes from the WTO agreement to open up the banking sector to genuine competition at the beginning of 2007. This agreement allows foreign banks to compete with domestic banks on a level playing field, accept local currency deposits and engage in the full range of corporate transactions.

Moreover, in addition to the lack of choice, life savings are deposited into state owned banks largely because the general population is not aware of the precarious financial position of these banks. These state institutions are all that many have known. If the bubble of misplaced confidence in these institutions (or the government) were pricked, and there were genuinely widespread and practical options to deposit savings into non-state owned institutions (such as foreign banks or a well functioning securities market) it's likely that a withdrawal of monies from state owned banks would occur on a massive scale, and bank liquidity would certainly be threatened. The regime's reluctance to promote genuine financial broadening—an increase in non-state owned banks and other forms of financial intermediaries such as stock markets and corporate bonds—is largely grounded in this fear of lost liquidity for the state owned banks. Even as China fulfils its WTO obligations by allowing foreign-owned and independent banks to receive deposits in local currency from individuals, foreign banks and analysts are in general agreement that the top priority of China's banking regulators is to protect the domestic market from foreign competition. This is being done through insistence on exorbitant capital requirements, slow licence approvals and other obstructive tactics.[87] If no alternative to state-owned banks remained it is debatable whether savings would be withdrawn on the same massive scale simply because there would be nowhere else to deposit the money. But if there was a massive 'bank run', which always occurs with immense speed, it is likely that crisis would hit before a central government could do much about it. As Gordon Chang puts it, 'In China there is no room for an adverse shock. A system that depends on the continual absence of bad news is by definition vulnerable.'[88]

If the regime can manage to maintain its dominance of the financial deposits sector and debt markets, then any unfolding loss of control is likely to be much slower. With over US$1 trillion in foreign reserves alone, there is a large pot of money to potentially conduct a few more cleanup operations and prop up the rickety system for a while longer. Official figures also stated that savings in mainland banks were US$3.7 trillion at the end of 2005, which means almost US$1.2 left over if we believe the official outstanding loans figure.[89] If these numbers are close to accurate, a collapse of the banking system may still be some time away. The regime could possibly continue the bailing-out and recapitalisation dance with the banks but their capacity to do so would decline over time as would the stimulus effect on growth.

It is also important to note that the decentralisation of political authority such as occurred in China exacerbates problems. In a study of the collapse of the Soviet Union, Steven Solnick demonstrated that decentralised authority tends to exacerbate the instances of the regime's misuse and theft of state assets.[90] In the case of China, this has certainly occurred. As decentralisation occurs in a one party system, the 'agents' of the state who remain unaccountable are multiplied. Where once there was a relatively small group of bureaucrats at the top controlling vast resources, there are now many more local bureaucrats controlling these same resources. The central leadership loses effective control and oversight over the agents (local bureaucrats) and the opportunities for theft of public resources, other opportunity costs of corruption, as well as the use of resources for non-productive 'political' purposes, multiply. Moreover, the renegotiation of rights and responsibilities between central and local CCP agents takes place mostly to the advantage of the latter. As local party members control and redistribute more resources, they are in a better position to use these resources to garner support for the regime, improve their local networks and connections, and in turn continue to demand support from the central leadership whose legitimacy relies more and more on the work and policies of local party officials. It is therefore difficult for the central leadership to both keep in touch with local issues and complaints and retake power and responsibility from local officials in any re-centralisation movement.

Can China trade its way out of trouble?

It is doubtful that China can trade its way out of trouble. Exports are already playing an important role as a growth driver, accounting for 12% of real GDP growth in 2004.[91] To put in perspective the Chinese reliance on foreign trade, while Chinese per capita GDP in 2005 was US$1,231, its per capita foreign trade volume was US$1,000 leaving non-trade related per capita income of only US$231.[92] As the World Bank's China Director, David Dollar, observed about China's export strategy:

> These numbers (export growth) are clearly not sustainable. China would have to carve out huge new external markets every year—markets already crammed with efficient producers across Asia, Europe and the United States—to keep this up.[93]

There is also something precarious about China's trade structure which relies overwhelmingly on US consumption and is hence extremely vulnerable to any decline in US consumption of Chinese exports. The US needs to effectively borrow over US$600 billion each year to fund its craving for imports. Only the most foolhardy believe that this can be maintained indefinitely. Thirty five percent of Chinese exports go to the US. Although the Chinese have a trade surplus of US$102 billion in 2005, without a trade surplus with the US, China would face a global trade deficit of about 6.25% of GDP, more than the United States' 5.7%. The point is that China is becoming too large to rely on export growth to pick up the slack of inefficient investment.

Moreover, the majority of FDI is being transferred to foreign owned companies in China that in turn use China as an export base. The latest figures indicate that foreign owned companies accounted for over 55% of China's exports in 2003 and 70% in 2005. This is not in itself a problem but the transfer of technologies and innovation to domestically owned businesses have been notoriously poor for various reasons.[94] For example, although China is able to export huge quantities of sophisticated electronics and information technology products, almost all of the high-value added parts are actually imported into China to be assembled. Hence, while China exported US$142 billion in high technology products in 2003, the import of these pre-assembled parts and components was about US$128 billion. In short, the net export of these high technology items was only US$14 billion, which moreover, was largely through wholly foreign owned firms operating in China.[95]

As a comparison, China received ten times more FDI than India in 2005 and about six times more in 2006. China has received over US$60 billion a year in FDI over the past three years. In 2006, the figure was US$63 billion.[96] Many take this as the global market's vote of confidence in the Chinese economy. Maybe so, but the billions of dollars in FDI entering China, and the billions of dollars in exports leaving China, are not having the transformative effect on its economy. This is because most of the FDI is designated for foreign owned firms while private domestic firms are prevented from competing in SOE dominated industries or are denied the capital needed to expand. As two highly regarded economists, Huang Yasheng and Tarun Khanna, Professors from the Sloan School of Management at the Massachusetts Institute of Technology and the Harvard Business School respectively, argue:

> China's export-led manufacturing boom is largely a creation of foreign direct investment, which effectively serves as a substitute for domestic entrepreneurship. During the last 20 years, the Chinese economy has taken off, but few local firms have followed, leaving the country's private sector with no world-class companies to rival the big multinationals.[97]

Conclusion

The Soviet experience revealed that the ability to mobilise resources does not mean that resources will be used efficiently. For authoritarian regimes controlling the vast bulk of the country's savings, the temptation to use resources for political ends is perhaps irresistible. Paul Krugman observed over a decade ago that 'current projections of Asian supremacy extrapolated from recent trends may well look almost as silly as 1960s-vintage forecasts of Soviet industrial supremacy did from the perspective of the Brezhnev years.'[98] As he further argues, even if economists lost sight of the impending Soviet economic demise, the Soviet decline could have been 'predicted on the basis of growth accounting.'[99]

Chinese leaders adopted the free market as a 'therapeutic' device to accelerate growth and remain in power. The regime never intended the free market to be transformative: 'limited government', 'property rights', 'rule of law' and so on. This is the politics driving the Chinese model. Steering a thriving economy from the seat of unchallenged power was Deng's grand plan. As Premier Wen declared recently, democracy would only develop once a 'mature socialist system' evolved and this could take 100 years.[100]

We need to look beyond China's headline growth figures because examining what lies behind them is not encouraging. The evidence suggests that commissioning the free market to further the rule of an authoritarian regime is riddled with perhaps fatal contradictions. The Chinese model cannot be sustained in its present form.

Part A
CHAPTER FOUR

Assessing 'Market Socialism'—
The Case for Pessimism

Chapter 4
Assessing 'Market Socialism'— The Case for Pessimism

Introduction

There was a brand of bicycle produced by China—the brand name is 'Forever'. It is a very heavy, very sturdy, but very ugly and very clumsy looking. It does not have much stylish decorations [sic] and looks very rusty ... The Chinese Communist Party is just like that brand of bicycle. First, it is very 'unstylish' and 'old fashioned'. It has vicious nicknames like 'commies' and 'chicoms'. Its gear and axis all look very ugly and are not even shiny under the sunlight, so you would not like to take your girlfriend out on such an embarrassing looking bicycle. But even though the Chinese Communist Party does not have such gadgets like elections, TV debates, free protests, political ads, etc, etc., it knows how to get things done ... It built China's first nuclear bomb, first automobile, first fighter jet, first nuclear submarine, first personal computer, etc. The Chinese Communist party is really a 'treasure-trove' in the hearts of the average Chinese family ... In conclusion, I want to praise the Chinese Communist Party some more. I think the Chinese people need not listen to those democracy lovers, and should totally ignore the flashy elections of America. The Chinese people have chosen the Chinese Communist Party, and we will continue to use that bicycle because we like it and there's nothing you can do about it. Maybe we'll renovate that bicycle once every few years, like putting on some new paint, or change an axle. But the bicycle is still the same old rusty bicycle. There's not a best bicycle in the world, there's only the most useful and practical bicycle.[1]

Math, *The Peking Duck* blog

The blog entry reproduced above represents the kind of defiant support that is growin—g for the Chinese model. Experts can debate the merits and flaws of models but the most compelling rhetorical argument that the Beijing Consensus has is the perception that it is working.

The evidence from the previous chapter shows that it is not working as well as official growth figures suggest. The Chinese regime has become skillful at partial imitation, selective adaptation and, increasingly, self-promotion. Glowing surveys of the Chinese economy by investment banks that are making millions from underwriting privatisation reforms and procuring capital for clients in an easy credit environment belie the difficulties of the grassroots situation and the meagreness of profits by most foreign and local firms.

At the expense of economic logic and efficiency, massive amounts of resources are being used to further social and political ends. But this is only part of the story with respect to the regime's problems. China stands a real risk of heading towards political and social turmoil. The regime's strategy of entrenching its legitimacy and rule through a 'therapeutic' free market is failing. Indeed, it is arguable that the mounting political and social deficits present a greater threat to the regime than its economic problems. Growth has not been the harbinger of social and political harmony that the leadership assumed. Certainly, the regime takes the reality of its declining legitimacy and the possibility of its own collapse much more seriously than many international observers appear to realise.

Holding onto power: a paranoid regime

Authoritarian regimes tend to be suspicious of elements within their populations at the best of times, but the CCP government is a fearful and paranoid regime. The gap between those benefiting from reform and those who are left behind is widening at a frightening pace. New elites are less interested in communist and revolutionary ideology, and more interested in material wealth. That new elites might demand greater freedom is a persistent concern for the regime. Those left behind may eventually feel abandoned by the Party. In this sense, the regime is fearful that support for it will slide from all sides.

Furthermore, recent history has not been kind to communist regimes. The leadership is fighting hard to avoid being the latest and most notable communist assignee to the 'scrapheap of history', as former US President Reagan once boldly predicted about the Soviet Union a decade before its fall. The CCP is struggling to persuasively redefine the next stage of Chinese socialism to an audience that is increasingly uninterested or disillusioned.

The signs suggesting a 'crisis of legitimacy' for the CCP are profound and widespread. This crisis springs from two sources. The first is an internal or domestic one; the second an external one.

(a) The crisis from within

'Revolution' was the cry that stirred the blood of the party's most ardent supporters—Mao with his ideas of entrenching 'permanent revolution', then 'continuous revolution', then his 'Great Leap Forward' and finally the disastrous 'Cultural Revolution'. Deng called his reforms 'China's Second Revolution'. The point is that establishing continuity from Mao onwards is mandatory rhetoric. 'Revolution' and forms of renewal have always been core to modern Chinese political story telling.

The problem for the CCP in modern times is that the rhetoric of revolution is no longer engaging. China has become less of a totalitarian state (where the state was deeply involved in every aspect of life) and more of an authoritarian one. As in all communities in which the fires of revolution have died, economic and material concerns assume greater importance. Opening up the economy has decreased the relevance of the CCP for millions of Chinese and increased the resentment of many others; in particular rural areas where reforms have been the most dramatic. Where once the Party was central to one's life from the cradle to death, for many it no longer provides such support. Importantly, the Party is failing to meet these political and social deficits which are growing at pace.

(i) Rural discontentment

Roughly half of the population still lives in rural areas where discontent is most evident. The leadership recognises the problem of rural discontentment but attributes the causes to the inevitable growing income gap as a result of the reform process. Indeed, that is how much of the world sees it and, ironically, rural income disparity is almost treated as comforting evidence for some that China is indeed reforming and modernising.

As noted earlier, research indicates that 80% of the Chinese that emerged out of poverty since 1978 did so in the first decade of reform. Since 1996, per capita income growth from agricultural activities has been generally declining and there was actually negative growth from 1998–2000.[2] Much of this was due to falling agricultural commodity prices and higher production costs which farmers do not always associate with the regime.

There is, however, growing evidence of deep resentment against taxes and fees levied against farmers known as 'peasant burdens'. Officially, such burdens cannot exceed 5% of net income. In reality, central laws do not stop local authorities from issuing their own levies, none of which are recorded in official statistics. Conservative estimates of local taxes and fees imposed range from 10–20% of net income,[3] to 30–40% of net income.[4] Moreover, these burdens tend to be regressive as such taxes are levied on a per capita basis. Hence, while poorer peasants (earning 400–500 yuan a year) paid about 17% in these taxes, those in the more wealthy coastal rural areas paid about 2.8% of their net income. When you consider, for example, that the average costs of production alone of the three main crops (rice, wheat and corn) are about 43% of the *sale* price, the local taxes in addition to federal ones, as well as other costs, the pressures on farmers are oppressive. A study done in 1999 in Hubei finding that farming in one jurisdiction was unprofitable for 80% of farmers is common.[5]

Besides the pure financial burden, the problem is that these taxes do not translate to government services such as infrastructure, public health and education—free services that were largely changed to user-pay ones during the reforms. Local taxes are therefore largely seen as illegitimate and self-serving for local Party members to preserve their relevance and position. This is brought out by various official and unofficial surveys that are cited in Pei's research. For example, in a survey of 2000 rural residents in Xinjiang in 2001, 'excessive tax burdens' were cited by 65% of respondents as the principal cause of social instability.

'Tax resistance' was prevalent in 40% of peasants surveyed. From the point of view of local authorities, collecting taxes and fees consumed 60–70% of their time. In one report issued by the National Bureau of Statistics in 2001, 70% of village party officials thought collecting these taxes was their 'most difficult task'.[6] In increasing numbers of cases, relations between local party officials and villages were so dysfunctional that officials relied on organised crime syndicates to aid in tax and fee collection through intimidation and violence.

Loyalty to the Party, and cooperation between it and rural China, is breaking down. As almost all instances of unrest in rural areas involve dissatisfaction with decisions or actions taken by local official bodies perceived to be corrupt or unfair, the CCP is explicitly implicated. Questionable land confiscations involving collusion between developers and local Party officials are common while 40 million peasants (and growing at about two million a year) have been forced off their land to make way for development without being given adequate compensation.[7] In China's fragmented system, the 'rent seeking' predation of local Party officials is politically, administratively and judicially unaccountable. Local officials extract 'rents' through their control of land, business regulations and other resources when the need arises.

All central attempts to solve this problem have been tactical rather than genuine. For example, the recent *feigaishui* reform to replace local fees with taxes (in order to reduce the arbitrariness of fee collection) was not accompanied by any moves to reduce the bloated size of rural government, nor any calls to account for their discretionary spending. While Premier Wen vowed to spend at least 340 billion yuan a year on rural infrastructure, education and health, such seemingly large amounts must be put in context with the fleets of cars for local officials that alone cost 300 billion yuan each year. Overseas trips, banquets and other entertainment costs incurred by these local officials cost about 500 billion yuan each year.[8] It is therefore not surprising that Wen's 2003 plan to abolish the town and rural township administrative levels (some 40,000 units) was abandoned due to immense opposition from vested interests within the CCP. The situation remains largely unchanged.

(ii) Unemployment

Although official Chinese figures tell us that unemployment and underemployment in urban areas are around the 5% mark and around 5–10% in rural areas, increasing numbers of independent studies (backed by anecdotal accounts) place urban and rural unemployment and underemployment at about 10–20% and 25–40% respectively.[9] Translated in human terms, this is between 125–200 million workers in rural areas, and 30–60 million workers in urban areas, struggling to find proper employment. Moreover, even during a sustained era of officially reported growth, a recent study found that for every 100 people in large and medium sized cities looking for jobs, there were only 65 on offer.[10] The argument that the millions of unhappy rural unemployed can be appeased simply by encouraging them to move to urban areas ignores this fact.

In a system with limited welfare protection, rising unemployment and the resulting unrest is feared by the CCP. Given the one-child policy and a widespread preference for having sons over daughters, some believe that the growing population of single unemployed men is a recipe for instability.[11] The desire to restrict unemployment is behind much of the logic to continually direct resources toward inefficient areas. However, the forced growth economy is not doing its job as far as employment is concerned. While the economy has been officially growing at close to 10% since 1980, employment growth fell from 4.2% in the 1980s to 1.1% in the 1990s.[12] Employment growth in the labour-absorbing non-agricultural sector declined from 6.8% in the 1980s to 3.4% in the 1990s.[13] By contrast, the working age population is growing at about 15%.

Although greater unemployment is the inevitable result of a planned economy in transition, the regime has only itself to blame for the severity of the problem. The regime is torn between laying-off workers to promote greater efficiency and instructing banks to offer more money to these organisations to keep them artificially alive. Any decision is taken on a case by case basis and is tactical rather than far-reaching. The difficulties are evident in several ways.

First, 'growing out of the plan' in terms of developing a world-class non-state sector alongside the public one has not been given the support that is needed. As mentioned, SOEs that similarly accounted for about a third of output received 70% of capital. Whereas profitable domestic private enterprises are best able to absorb workers in productive and sustainable ways (and raise their incomes at the same time), they have been relatively starved of state capital. Indeed, the percentage of private firms receiving bank loans in the 1990s was actually lower than in the 1980s; by the early 1990s, informal finance substantially overtook bank finance for private firms.[14] Although the number of private firms has grown consistently, this poor access to the overwhelming majority of China's capital has limited the growth of many of these profitable private firms beyond a certain size. The median size of private firms in the 1990s actually remained the same as that of the 1980s, at about 30 employees.[15] The absence of giant, world class Chinese private firms is telling. Despite the 'economic miracle', there is not one Chinese equivalent of a world class corporate brand like Toyota or Samsung that has emerged out of China. As one Chinese commentator notes, 'Though governments at all levels have attached great importance to the development of private firms in their statements, such firms still felt the inequality in government treatment when compared with state-owned and foreign-invested enterprises.'[16] What this means is that the domestic private sector has been unable to absorb the mass of rural economic migrants searching for jobs in urban areas. Growth of employment in the non-state sector fell from 6.8% in the 1980s to 3.4% in the 1990s.[17] For every 65 that find one, 35 do not. With an estimated 200 million excess rural workers throughout China, and about 140 million 'floating' workers on the move and looking for jobs, the solution to move them into the cities is not a viable one.

Second, research shows that the same volume of capital hires less labour in China than in other developing countries.[18] This flows from the mass capital allocation to SOEs that is designed to preserve jobs, not create them. Moreover, with the failure rate of Chinese investment projects remaining at about 50% from 1958–2001,[19] and with a failure rate for medium and large-scale projects at 42% from 1991–1995, such waste of capital is hardly conducive to employment creation.

Third, in the quest for growth at all costs, little attention or resources are reserved for alleviating the effects of unemployment.

Laid-off workers experience an immediate and drastic decline in living standards. According to one survey, for men who were laid-off, unemployment payments and social welfare constituted only 7.9% of post-employment support, with savings and income of another family member contributing to the lion's share at 57%.[20] This is indicative of other surveys.[21]

As evidence of mass unemployment mounts, few workers see the government or the Party as a saviour. The Party is irrelevant at best, and has betrayed them at worse. Various surveys bring this out. For example, in Tianjin, only 2.3% of laid-off workers indicated they would rely on government support. In Changchun, only 5% would count on the government to solve their economic problems. Not surprisingly, in a 1999 survey, 70% of laid-off workers said they were dissatisfied with their lives and 75% of them sympathised with workers staging collective demonstrations.[22]

(iii) Neglecting social goods and safety nets

For a 'socialist' regime system in transition toward a 'market socialist' system, the lack of resources saved for social or public goods is a ticking time-bomb for the regime.

For example, while life expectancy has risen dramatically to 71 years in 2003—largely the result of disease prevention measures—the country's medical insurance system covers fewer than 50% of urban residents and about 10% of rural residents.[23] About 90% of rural residents were covered in the 1970s. Since the government only spends about 15% of the health budget on rural areas, public health is deteriorating quickly. Rural residents rely largely on 'village clinics', in which 40% of practitioners in one survey were found to be not registered, two-thirds of practitioners did not keep medical records, and only half of injection tubes and needles were sterilised.[24] Even in urban areas, 44% of residents who were sick declined to go to hospital in 2003 because of rising healthcare costs.[25]

Moreover, although China's ageing population is common knowledge—China will get old before they get rich is the cliché—only 55% of urban workers and 11% of rural workers are covered by the pension systems.[26] These pension obligations appear to be another 'black hole' in China's mismanaged financial system. In 2002, consultants McKinsey & Co released a report stating that China's 'pay as you go' pension pools 'were on the verge of bankruptcy';[27] not surprising as the system is based on employers making enough profit to meet these obligations. Although the Chinese suggest a US$100–200 billion problem (using official employment figures), others like the World Bank and Lehman Brothers investment bank put it at about US$1 trillion in 2002.[28] Since then it has got worse. Mass forced retirement might make the unemployment figures look good but puts further stress on an already broken down pension system. By 2030, about a quarter of the population will be over sixty compared to 10% currently. That will be almost 350 million people.

We could list dozens of areas that have deteriorated despite the impressive growth figures—from fair access to judicial and administrative resolution, to environmental and water degradation, to sewage, to rural roads, to working traffic lights and so on. The important point is that there have been very poor attempts to replace the 'cradle to grave' benefits of the 'iron rice bowl' and resentment is festering as Chinese residents repeatedly hear about China's world-beating growth rates.

Much of the problem lies in China's dysfunctional fiscal system. As the capacity of provincial and local authorities to collect taxes and fees increases, social spending is increasingly neglected and spending becomes more unaccountable. Why? In 1978, the government's tax receipts were about 30% of GDP while in 1999 figures, it was about 14% of GDP. This figure, however, is augmented by about 20% of off-budget and unrecorded revenues mainly collected by provincial and local governments in the form of taxes and fees. In other words, the proportion of government revenues has remained constant at about 30% but most of it is now controlled by local and provincial governments. These local and provincial governments have little interest in spending to receive 'social returns', cannot be called into account for these 'unrecorded' revenues, and hence have complete discretion. They are more likely to spend the money on big 'growth' projects which have higher political returns and can offer tangible 'economic' growth results than on social goods that are harder to measure and extract praise for.

(iv) The crisis of legitimacy

As the regime fails to distribute the fruits of transition fairly or wisely, it is not surprising that a crisis of legitimacy is already looming. The rural situation is particularly troubling for the CCP. Official claims last released in 1998 put poverty at 4.8% in rural areas which is somewhere over 40 million people in human terms.[29] Using international standards of poverty measurement, the World Bank estimates the poverty level is more than double the official one at 12–15% or around 106 million people in poverty.[30]

The upshot has been a drastic decline in the Party's legitimacy in these areas. An internal report in the mid 1990s found that up to 75% of rural Party organisations were in a 'state of collapse'.[31] A report by the Shanxi CCP branch in 2000 admitted that 700 villages had not recruited a single member in the previous three years. This is far from atypical. Between 1994 and 2000, the CCP was forced to 'fix' 356,000 rural CCP cells—the most important grassroots political entities—that were adjudged to be 'weak' or 'paralysed'. This represented half of the CCP's village cells. This is consistent with reports from the Shanxi, Zhejiang and Sichuan Provincial Organisation Departments (PODs) that over half the village cells in these regions were in serious trouble. A survey of CCP members in Sichuan showed that one in four did not support or trust the party and wanted to end their membership.[32]

Although the rural situation is of greatest concern, the urban situation is also serious. There has been a direct correlation between closures and bankruptcies of SOEs, and the effective dismantling or crippling of CCP infrastructure in those areas. This is not surprising as SOEs were at the heart of local party activities. For example, in Liaoning which was one of the provinces hardest hit by SOEs closures in the 1990s, 80,000 CCP members were among the 680,000 workers employed in those factories. Of the 80,000, only 8% subsequently re-applied for party activity passes, and the rest effectively voluntarily surrendered contact with the CCP.[33] Similarly, in an internal report prepared by the Shanxi CCP POD, the conclusion was that 'in non-operating SOEs, the party organisation is almost in a state of collapse. It does not conduct organisational activities or recruit new members. It cannot even collect party dues.'[34]

As these insights are taken from official provincial CCP research, we can be certain the leadership is aware of them. They are serious enough to fuel paranoia in any authoritarian regime. There is, however, more evidence of widespread disenchantment with the CCP. In a survey of over 800 migrant rural workers in Beijing in 1997–1998, only 5% thought that local cadres 'worked for the interests of the villages and do not use their power for private gains.' Some 60% said that local cadres '*only* use their power for private gains and *do not* work for the interests of the villages.' Eighty-five percent said that village heads (who are CCP members) and CCP secretaries were corrupt.[35]

Consider now the instances of unrest and protest in China.[36] These have grown from a few thousand in the early 1990s to 58,000 instances in 2003 to 87,000 in 2005[37] involving an estimated 4.5 to 15 million people. As these are official figures, it is almost certain that the number is greater than that stated. For example, a Hong Kong based labour rights group estimated that the figure was closer to 300,000 protests in 2003.[38] Moreover, as one report to US Congress affirms, 'Although political observers have described social unrest among farmers and workers since the early 1990s, recent protest activities have been broader in scope, larger in average size, greater in frequency and more brash than those a decade ago.'[39]

The vast majority of these protests are directed toward CCP officials and policies: laid-off SOE workers, urban development displacing homes without adequate compensation, arbitrary and corrupt rulings by local CCP officials, repressive tactics by local officials to implement decisions and policies and so on.

Although these rising instances of protests are not generally politically motivated and are not organised or unified, they clearly represent growing dissatisfaction with the CCP. In other words, they bring to light the 'crisis of legitimacy' that is plaguing the party. Although the party has given extensive thought to dealing with these protests in a way that mitigates escalation of unrest— which essentially involves either brutally targeting the organisers but exercising restraint on the use of force against the majority of protesters, or paying off organisers or aggrieved protesters to defuse the situation—the point is that having a monopoly on the organs of force and enforcement has never been enough. The party is failing to provide for the people in modern times what they once provided and the result is that the CCP is becoming irrelevant at best, and resented at worst.

The CCP is fearful, but it is probably justified in being paranoid as well. These are seriously troubling developments for any authoritarian regime, and certainly for one that rules over 1.3 billion people. The further problem is that the regime does not know which pocket of dissatisfaction or resistance could spring into something bigger and therefore seeks to suppress all forms of alternative thought and activity as much as possible. The regime's repression of the Falun Gong movement is a perfect example. Many in the West fail to understand why the regime would care about a movement which is not political in nature and preaches 'truthfulness', 'benevolence' and 'forbearance'. In its current paranoid mindset, any movement with millions of followers that is separate from the regime presents a danger, especially one led by a charismatic leader in the form of Li Hongzhi. Officially accused of 'engaging in illegal activities, advocating superstition and spreading fallacies, hoodwinking people, inciting and creating disturbances, and jeopardising social stability',[40] religion and organised belief systems seriously needle the CCP's paranoia. The role of Pope John-Paul II in helping to inspire the drive to end communism in Eastern Europe provides a chilling historical lesson for the Chinese regime and it is no coincidence that the only 'Catholic' worship allowed in China is that under the auspices of the Chinese Patriotic Catholic Association (CPCA), a division of Beijing's Religious Affairs Bureau.

(b) The crisis from without

The second source for a crisis of legitimacy springs from an external one and it is one the CCP are extremely fearful about. Chinese politicians speak frequently and enthusiastically about how excited they are by opportunities arising from 'globalisation'. The mantra is particularly well received by Western business leaders. However, it is clear that the CCP is ambivalent about China entering a globalised world which they consider a 'double edged sword'.[41] On the one hand, the economic pay-off is unmistakable. On the other, outside influences are likely to fuel greater questioning of CCP authority and policies—especially by the rising middle classes who are prospering from the modern reforms. In particular, greater access to information through the Internet and television inevitability mean that the population will learn more and more about international and Western norms, as well as gain a deeper appreciation of China's problems such as income disparity, corruption and fundamental economic difficulties.

A more affluent and educated population with greater access to information is also a serious threat to the regime's control and manipulation of its official histories. Controlling the telling of history is important in establishing the entitlement of the Party to rule. For example, state sanctioned historians tell the story of how China's ruling Party has brought dignity, unity and order to China after its 150 years of humiliation. Chinese textbooks teach students that the defeat of the Japanese in the Second World War was the result of the Mao led Communist resistance, and not due to the Americans dropping the bomb on Hiroshima and Nagasaki. Many young Chinese do not know about the Party's role in the chaos and organised violence of the Cultural Revolution, which in the name of strengthening China killed millions of Chinese, destroyed the education system and paralysed the economy.[42] What they are told instead is that 'Mao called for political participation and got a national riot'[43]—a clear edict against democratisation. The attempts to censor international television and news programs and the 'Golden Shield' initiative with its over 30,000 state employees working to block and censor websites from well over 100 million Chinese Internet users—known by outsiders as the 'Great Firewall of China'—must be understood in this light.[44]

In trouble with its own people

In a survey of workers in Beijing in 1998, two thirds of respondents thought the authority of local cadres were 'low' or 'very low', 60% believed their authority was declining and 85% believed their village heads and CCP secretaries were corrupt.[45]

Behind China's official world beating growth rates, the government's place in society is tenuous, and the tensions between the regime and the population are increasing. The leadership had named 'domestic stability' achieved by a 'well-off society' (*xiaokang shehui*) as its single biggest challenge. The CCP has hedged their bets unwisely and China's growth, unsustainable in any case, has come at a huge political cost. The regime is losing its appeal, its rationale to exist and rule exclusively is weak, its capacity to garner and mobilise support is declining, and its organisation is fragmenting. The Party is no longer able to build broad-based coalitions and instead has to rely on increasingly desperate and burgeoning tactical redistribution policies to remain in power. In a story typical of authoritarian regimes long after the fires of revolution have died, it is seen as corrupt, self-serving, and perhaps worse of all for an authoritarian regime, increasingly ineffectual and irrelevant. For a regime that tries to combine the role of 'defender of the socialist faith' as well as 'free market reformer', the contradictions mean that they have succeeded in neither.

With its traditional rural support base in tatters, resentment of urban populations growing, and new elites agreeing to be co-opted only while there is more money to be made, the leadership is fretfully delaying the consequences of its wasteful resource allocation policies. Meanwhile, the economic, social and political deficits accumulate. The government is not meeting the terms of its 'social contract' and fulfilling the necessary functions that legitimate governments must fulfil to remain in power. For a one-Party authoritarian regime, this obligation is even more critical and the standards more onerous.

Some might predict an incremental slowdown in growth rates given China's flawed model but few are brave enough to predict the actual or effective breakdown of the regime. However, even a modest slowdown would have significant social and political effects and the ingredients are all there for a potential social or political meltdown.

The drying of the reservoir

In an eloquent piece on the rise of China viewed from the Chinese perspective, editor of *Time* magazine, Michael Elliott, observed:

> Most casual observers outside China don't understand that even as the nation gains respect, its people are haunted by a deep sense of past slights. China's long journey toward modernity began not because the dragon gently flexed its scaly muscles but because others prodded it with a sharp stick. When China

began to open up to the world 150 years ago, it did so because gun-ships of the British Royal Navy, working in the service of opium smugglers, forced the imperial government to accept foreign trade. As China sees its history, the country was subjected to foreign humiliation for the next century, its territory invaded and dismembered, its people raped and massacred. Along with the foreign interventions came homegrown catastrophes: rebellions, revolutions, civil wars, famine and unspeakable cruelty. *Luan*, the Chinese word for chaos, is perhaps the single most important concept that the outside world needs to grasp about the new China, for the memory of the long years of chaos continues to have a profound impact on Chinese thinking today.[46]

The reservoir is deep and the CCP draws heavily from this collective yearning for dignity to be returned to the Chinese people. The Party is the custodian of this sacred assignment. It tells its people that it will bring stability and prosperity, and return China to greatness. Yet, a sense of mission and a sense of entitlement is not the same thing. The mission of the CCP was to lead China back from chaos to greatness. But its sense of entitlement to rule has taken over. Hanging onto power at any cost has become its overwhelming concern. A failing political-economy model accompanied by mounting economic, social and political deficits is the result. Co-opting new elites and appeasing older ones is done through material means. Even relatively small decreases in economic growth would have dramatic results. Even the deepest reservoirs without refilling eventually dry out.

Conclusion

In the past 20 years and more since China embarked on the road of reform and opening up, we have moved steadfastly to promote political restructuring and vigorously build democratic politics under socialism.

President Hu's speech to Australian Parliament,
24 October 2003

97

Protesters mocked President Bush for America's human rights failings yet remained silent when the Chinese President came for a visit a day later. Indeed, President Hu was given the honour of a standing ovation by Parliament after his speech. Perhaps Australians are too reluctant to offend Chinese sensibilities even though President Hu's vigorous building of 'democratic politics under socialism' sits squarely with La Rochefoucauld's adage that hypocrisy is vice paying homage to virtue. The CCP retains organised power for itself through repression and at the expense of any other party or grouping. Democratic politics under socialism is more about voting processes within the Party than elections that are genuinely contested. Experimental elections at almost one million villages somehow contrive to have unpopular CCP officials voted back into office. Use of the term 'democratic' is an empty gesture on the part of the regime. As Deng openly admitted in dismissing democracy:

> The purpose of reforming the system of the Party and state leadership is precisely to maintain and further strengthen Party leadership and discipline, and not to weaken or relax them. In a big country like ours, it is inconceivable that unity of thinking could be achieved among several hundred million people ... Without such a Party, our country would split up and accomplish nothing.[47]

In more recent times, President Hu leaves us in no doubt that he seeks to continue this tradition:

> The Communist Party of China takes a dominant role and coordinates all sectors ... The leading position of the Party is a result of a long-term practice and is clearly stipulated by the Constitution ... The role of the Party organisations and Party members in government departments should be brought into full play so as to realise the Party's leadership over state affairs.[48]

The tragedy is that this determination to remain in power and remain dominant in all affairs is at the heart of China's problems.

The originator of the Beijing Consensus, Ramo, argued that Beijing had introduced 'a new physics of development and power.' Instead, Beijing's attempts to live in a parallel universe where the form of free markets is accepted but much of the substance and logic of it (which calls for curbs on the role and power of government) is not. Ramo also argued that the flexible model allowed the Chinese to fit into the global system 'in a way that allows them to be truly independent [and] to protect their way of life', and to pursue an 'equitable model of development.' Instead, behind the Beijing Consensus is a regime desperate to hold onto its authoritarian rule by using the fruits of the partial free market system to entrench its power. Finally, where 'gradualism' and 'flexibility' is promoted as a virtue, it is in reality the strategy adopted by authoritarian regimes to buy time to build new footings when the country is forced to modernise and change.

The Chinese Model is far less 'nimble' and 'robust' than optimists like Keidel suggest.

Most analysts offer advice on security and foreign policy based on China's rise. It is worthwhile asking what challenges we might face vis-à-vis a China that is stagnating, declining or, in the worst case, imploding. The decline of China is not inevitable. But I argue that its current model of political-economy is untenable and unsustainable. The model needs a significant overhaul and the most important reforms (and the most serious obstacles to them) are largely political rather than economic. If left unchanged - as is appearing increasingly likely - the case for pessimism is strong. The mounting economic, political and social deficits have placed enormous pressure on the regime.

Part B will look at possible developments within Chinese politics and resulting challenges we face vis-à-vis a stagnating, declining or imploding China rather than an increasingly prosperous and rising one.

Part B
CHAPTER ONE

The Internal and External Consequences
of Declining Legitimacy

PART B

Chapter 1
The Internal and External Consequences of Declining Legitimacy

Introduction

Failing states and failing regimes present many different challenges to meeting the rise of successful states and successful regimes; a fortiori when talking about a great power. China evidently needs peace and stability to continue its development. But its 'peaceful rise' follows the logic of a successful state in transition. Yet, the predominant driving force of an unsuccessful state or regime in transition might very well take a different and less predictable form. In particular, the Peoples' Liberation Army remains a critical factor in the future direction of Chinese politics and society. The dynamics of transition with respect to relations between the CCP-PLA and segments of the population are ever evolving. And in the event of an unsettled and failing transition, likely troubling.

What factors are building towards the *possibility* of a failing Chinese state, or more precisely, a failing Chinese regime? I have pointed to four interrelated factors in the preceding chapters. The first is the crisis of legitimacy that is deepening for the CCP. The second is the vertical fragmentation of power and the declining ability to implement and execute top-down macro policy because of the shift in power, economic control and resources toward local authorities. The third is unsound economics. The fourth is a regime increasingly failing to meet the social needs and expectations of huge numbers of its people—a serious failing in an authoritarian system such as China's.

Crucially, despite the best efforts of the CCP, these are also challenges that established liberal democracies are generally able to address more effectively given greater levels of social and political accountability and debate, and the greater structural alignment of interests between polities and regimes. The timeless stuff of politics—'obligation' and 'coercion' according to Isaiah Berlin—and economics—the creation, use and distribution of wealth and resources—is not functioning well in authoritarian China. These are the on-the-ground realities that China keeps quiet from the world while others enthusiastically proclaim the miracle of China's stellar rise.

Despite these problems, no one really knows where or what China will be in ten or 20 years' time. Consequently, no one can be certain about the most appropriate strategy for the 'China question'. At best, recent history provides only limited lessons on how we should deal with China. China is neither Nazi Germany nor the Soviet Union. There is no certainty that it is a modern version of Bismarck's Germany. 'Containment' appears too extreme and unnecessarily provocative; and given China's role in the global economy, few countries would be prepared to support a containment policy. Simple 'engagement' seems too optimistic. China provides an emerging hard and soft power challenge to America and the West. Beijing's focus on 'comprehensive national power' includes a combination of international prestige, economic and military power, cultural influence, and regional leadership. An 'engagement' policy that ignores these challenges would be irresponsible. Further, an engagement policy that blissfully assumes China can be managed or pressured to democratise, or that democratisation is inevitable, is similarly misguided. Finally, forceful intervention is out of the question. It would be, by some margin, the most reckless and ill-advised approach that could be taken.

Even though a comprehensive strategy to deal with China is in doubt, since China's future is still unclear, many analyses are premised on China's inevitable rise. The more optimistic viewpoints such as those put forward by Zheng Bijian[1] and Kishore Mahbubani[2] are premised on China's continued 'peaceful rise' or 'peaceful development'. The term 'peaceful rise' was first used by Chinese leaders in 2003 to counter international fears about Beijing's growing power. The argument was that China needed a peaceful environment and good relations with other powers to focus on its economic development. Its rise would therefore be peaceful rather than disruptive. As Premier Wen Jiabao declared in 2004:

China's rise will not come at the cost of any other country, will not stand in the way of any other country, nor pose a threat to any other country.[3]

The 'peaceful rise' thesis is essentially based on two arguments. First, China's transition from a backward to a prosperous nation will be a successful one; and second, the benefits of peace will outweigh the gain from conflict during this transition.

Part A argued that China's current political-economy model is flawed and failing. Although the future is far from certain, without further political reform, China's continued rise is very much open to question. Therefore, assuming that China will continue to reform successfully is as much a matter of guesswork as predicting a China that will fail to adequately reform. This part looks at possible consequences of a struggling and increasingly desperate regime both domestically and with respect to key aspects of China's foreign relations. In particular, how the regime might respond to mounting economic, political and social pressure in the quest to hold onto power—whether the benefits of peace will always outweigh the benefits of conflict—is an important question.

Condition precedents

Speculation about a declining or even failing China must be based on a series of 'condition precedents' that might or might not occur. Even if China does not undertake significant political reform, lessons from the Ottoman and Hapsburg Empires to the Soviet Union teach that even systems with deep and inherent flaws (that we now know about) can exist for a surprisingly long time and need to be pushed by exceptional (or sometimes just the seemingly innocuous) historical incidents and events before falling over. Some regimes can also delay the onset of significant decline through partial adaptation and reinvention. However, I argue that while political reform remains stunted, these 'condition precedents' for failure are firming up and it is time to give serious thought to what a failing Chinese regime might look like and how such a regime might respond. Although such speculation will always invite criticism and counter-scenarios, there are some troubling trends emerging in China.

Individual personalities have historically been important in understanding Chinese politics and decision-making at the top. The larger-than-life figures of Mao and Deng exercised more power and discretion than their official positions and titles suggested. Since then, leadership has been weakly institutionalised and while the current leader of the 'Fourth Generation', Hu, lacks the stature of Mao or Deng, his position as 'paramount leader' is entrenched as President, Party leader and, more recently, Chairman of the Central Military Commission (CMC). Nevertheless, to remain in power, President Hu needs the support of both dominant factions within the CCP and the loyalty of the PLA.

Part A looked at the economic challenges. But President Hu's authority and position within the Party, as well as the larger question of the regime's future, will also largely depend on how well Hu and his successors meet the political and social challenges facing the regime. As I will outline below, these challenges are much more serious than many commentators in the West realise. The two recent trends that need to be discussed are the emergence of the 'New Left' in Chinese politics under President Hu's leadership and the dynamics of CCP-PLA relations in the context of these profound political and social challenges for the regime. Domestic pressures influence foreign policy. The following chapter will then look at how these domestic concerns, and the regime's responses to them, are loosening the foundations of a foreign policy that could very well be different to the one behind China's 'peaceful rise'.

Between order and chaos—political and social challenges for the regime

One of the writers that best understood the phenomenon of totalitarianism in the twentieth century, Robert Conquest, argues that any totalitarian attempt to control all aspects of life is untenable in the long run and allowing a far greater leeway on some matters—'tactical disagreements'—is much more viable.[4]

China is no longer a totalitarian state. The regime no longer seeks to control every aspect of life or way of thinking. Although the CCP remains determined to hold onto power, there is no 'utopian' end-goal as such that totalitarian regimes ruthlessly strive toward. Indeed, as I have argued, the Party is becoming less relevant to many Chinese and different forms of behaviour are largely tolerated as long as it is not deemed to be threatening to CCP authority or social stability. In the words of one expert who has worked and lived in China for over 25 years, 'life in China has softened a great deal'.[5]

This might augur well for the regime if it were not suffering an immense 'crisis of legitimacy'. Many former totalitarian regimes like the one in the Soviet Union became most vulnerable when they were in transition. This makes sense since regimes are only 'totalitarian' in nature when they can be. Single party systems reach their heights when their vision of the future is universally received and there is sufficient 'buy-in' from the population for the regime to employ totalitarian tactics, of which state-backed force is only one part of the coercive apparatus. When regimes move toward softer authoritarian models, it is often a sign that their grip on society is slipping and they have no choice but to relax aspects of authority.

Political and social challenges are mounting. For the CCP, the current transitional period is correctly seen as a period of immense significance in terms of the future of its authoritarian rule in China.

(a) The credibility problem for the regime

There is growing evidence that the authority and capacity of the regime to govern (in addition to its legitimacy) are declining. This is occurring for two main reasons.

First, although it is now clear that increasingly allowing the operation of free markets was seen as 'therapeutic' rather than 'transformative in terms of Chinese politics and society', the authority of the CCP is now based on an insecure strategy of inefficiently using resources to fuel a bubble economy. Moreover, the solution—to grant the private sector greater and greater access to this wealth and control of critical sectors of the economy—would accelerate the irrelevance of the Party and heighten the ability to remain exclusively in power. As the regime continues to oversee an economy based on unsound fundamentals and becomes increasingly less able to provide social and public goods, more and more cracks appear in the façade of CCP credibility. The survey results we cited in the previous chapter bring this out emphatically.

Second, public decision-making and administration becomes more sporadic and unpredictable as the disconnect between the central leadership and the majority of its population becomes more pronounced. This is occurring for several reasons. First, senior CCP members are increasingly becoming part of the new wealthy elites as a result of their privileged position within a China growing richer. Moreover, as part of the tactic to co-opt the new and emerging urban elites, the senior leadership has neglected the poor and especially rural populations to their detriment. It is easy to forget that there are still about 900 million rural inhabitants in China (and only 100–150 million in the middle and upper classes). The capacity (and intent) of the leadership to understand their problems and deal with their complaints is greatly diminished. Second, as the regime decentralised, there was a resulting loss of fiscal (tax collection and spending), administrative and legislative power for the central government which was increasingly transferred to local ones. This means that the execution of political, social, legal or economic macro policy from the top becomes much more difficult and unpredictable. In other words, there is a loss of centralised control and a greater reliance on local governments that are neither very accountable nor transparent. The worse local government practices tend to be in the poorer rural areas which are ruled by the 'law of local leaders'.

The lack of predictability might be less important in a purely agrarian society of uneducated peasants shut off from the world and each other but is much more critical as a society becomes more complex and the people more educated. China has a literacy rate of about 80% which includes most of the poor peasants. Looking at the Soviet experience, Alfred Evans argued that the inability to set up impartial mechanisms for adjudication, enforcement and regulation, and effective rules for resolving disputes, went a long way towards explaining the resulting loss of legitimacy for the regime and the subsequent implosion of the system.[6] If simple grievances like why one is prohibited from bidding for a legitimate contract in a neighbouring province, or why one's home can be bulldozed without warning or adequate compensation despite national laws stating otherwise, are not resolved in an appropriate and predictable way, daily life is invariably compromised and the regime is invariably blamed. In one study, of the 10 million petitions registered in 2003 with the Petitions Office, erected to hear and resolve public grievances and disputes, just two out of every thousand were resolved.[7] If the one Party in power retains the right to 'intervene' regardless of agreed rules and does so either because of a fragmented and disjointed decision-making process, or else because of politically motivated or corrupt CCP officials, the tactic of central leadership deflecting blame towards local officials starts to wear thin. If the CCP maintains that 'it knows best' and the rule-of-law can be bypassed by incompetent or corrupt CCP officials as well as courts and tribunals ultimately under the Party's instruction, then the loss of credibility remains directed towards the Party as a whole.

The fact that the reported instances of unrest are rising exponentially obviously suggests a rising tide of discontent. However, beyond this, most analyses stop there since little information is revealed by the government about the nature of these instances and what they concern. What we mostly hear from the Chinese government is talk of 'procedures' established to mitigate the seriousness of these incidents. Piecing together a picture of what is happening has mostly been left to intrepid insiders and determined reporters. These piecemeal reports, that are becoming more lucid and comprehensive, point to scenarios that have variously been described as a 'tipping point', 'time bomb' and a 'precipice' for the regime. Indeed, official media channels can no longer hide (and perhaps no longer want to hide) the rising instances of social unrest. These instances are the most tangible signs of a more and more disgruntled population.

(b) Social unrest in China

Officially reported instances of social unrest (involving 15 or more people) have risen from 8,700 in 1993 to 87,000 in 2005 (the latest available figures). This is about 240 instances each day.

The first important point about the rising instances of social unrest is that it indicates a citizenry that is increasingly defiant or unafraid of the authoritarian coercive apparatus. This means either that the level of discontent is so profound that the protestors no longer care about the consequences of unrest or that the regime's ability to enforce compliance and order has been seriously compromised. As the truth is undoubtedly a combination of both, this is worrying news for any authoritarian government.

Second, although indicators are that millions have been saved from poverty under World Bank standards of one dollar a day, this statistic must be tempered by the fact that social and financial safety nets (such as, health, education and welfare) have been greatly reduced during the reform period. For example, a recent UN study estimated that out-of-pocket spending on healthcare in China has almost doubled as a percentage of total health expenditure from 1980 to 2002 from 36% to 68%. Meanwhile, government spending in the same period has been reduced from 32% to 15%.[8] Much progress was made from 1979 to the mid-1980s. Since then, of the approximately 900 million peasants, about 400 million have seen their incomes stagnate or decline during the past decade.[9]

Third, the political danger is not just the growing divide between China's minority 'privileged classes' and the rest (most of which are desperately poor)—although this is in itself a genuinely tragic humanitarian crisis[10]—but the fact that most of the cases, and the worst cases, of unrest are directed towards local authorities and officials. In other words, the problem is seen to emanate from the government and a connection is made between the regime and the hardships the general population face. This is not surprising since most cases involve frustrations caused by corrupt officials, arbitrary and repressive taxes and land grabs from officials, unpaid benefits or loss of rights against official bodies, non-enforcement of laws by authorities and courts, lay-offs of workers by the state, use of thugs by local officials to demand compliance, and the like. Even though they control about two thirds of government revenue collection (with the central government receiving about a third), local officials do not deliver services that are relied upon by the masses because of insufficient budgeting, corruption or incompetence. When local officials want more money, they simply collect more taxes or fees. In rural areas, because all village land is ostensibly collectively owned, the lack of clear and definable property rights allows greedy local officials to effectively make decisions as to how the land is used, distributed, sold, developed and so on. The regime is intrinsically culpable. The frustrations cannot be dismissed as unruly citizens fighting among themselves or as a result of racial or intra-provincial tensions as the central leadership attempts to do.

Fourth, the size of instances of unrest is growing and can be frightening. For example, in cases recently documented for 2003, a mob of 50,000 torched police cars in Chongqing to protest the beating of a migrant worker; 100,000 stormed a government building and forced the postponement of a dam project in Sichuan due to inadequate compensation; 20,000 miners and their families rioted against layoffs and the loss of their pensions.[11] Other recent instances of unrest include 80,000 retired workers who protested in China's northeast over unpaid pensions in 2002; 30,000 rioting over exorbitant bridge tolls issued by local authorities in 2004; 7000 textile workers protesting after being forbidden to form their own union in the Shaanxi Province in 2004.[12] Of the 74,000 instances recorded in 2004, 17 involved 10,000 or more people, 46 involved 5,000 or more people and 120 involved 1,000 or more people. That order was only restored only after martial law was implemented in many of these cases highlights the seriousness of the problem. Even for the smaller incidents, the numerous anecdotal accounts of protestors violently targeting or resisting authorities speaks volumes about the crumbling regard for the 'peoples' party.

The government strategy of linking their legitimacy to macro economic growth might temporary placate the privileged classes but has no apparent bearing at all on reducing social unrest. As the Chinese economy boomed from 2001–2005, the number and scale of incidents continued to rise—further evidence as if more were needed—that the fruits of any growth are restricted to the privileged few.[13] Clearly, impressive macro figures inflated by fixed investment spending cannot solve problems festering away in the micro environment.

(c) The possibility of coordinated social unrest

When speculating about the future, there is no way to know to what extent something is 'possible' or 'probable'. This would require perfect knowledge of who, what, where, how and why.

This is the inherent incomprehensibility of (knowing) causation in any human activity—particularly so when dealing with the world's most populous nation. We can, however, point to certain *condition precedents* that, should they occur, would make events more likely or more unlikely.

We do know that China is a country in a profound mess. Its economics and wealth creation are inefficient and flawed, its financial structure is unsound, and the misallocation of resources is massive, chronic and deep-rooted. Its growth is artificially fuelled and unsustainable, and the wealth created is systematically wasted and directed towards less and less productive areas. Government and social deficits are mounting while the regime—which is itself largely the cause of them—cannot offer any viable solutions for them without precipitating its own demise. It therefore maintains a holding strategy while these problems worsen. Meanwhile, the lot of the majority of the population is either stagnant or in decline, while economic elites (who are the regime's newest support base) continue to thrive but only as a result of the tenuous and ultimately unsustainable growth strategy. Most significant decisions made by the regime are therefore tactical ones—putting out spot fires—driven by the logic of pure political survival rather than the logic of fundamental and sustainable transformation. Meanwhile, the fragmented regime hangs on the best it can and eliminates or impedes any threats they can see to their political dominance.

Most commentators outside China agree that the possibility of coordinated and widespread social unrest is low and does not pose any foreseeable threat to the regime. Although the social unrest is usually directed toward local officials and, by implication, the regime as a whole, it is not coordinated. They do not generally call for the overthrow of the CCP let alone constitute any kind of pro-democratic movement, and they do not amount to, in the eyes of most experts, a Tiananmen-style protest that is aimed at the central leadership. They are probably better understood as unprompted pressure valves to vent and release frustrations within a system that does not provide formal mechanisms for such release. They tend to be reactive rather than political in nature and many believe that a social movement arising from one of them appears unlikely.

However, the confidence many Western commentators have that these protests do not contain the seeds of coordinated mutiny is of little comfort to the Chinese leadership who take this possibility much more seriously. It is true that there is no ready-made and credible political alternative to the CCP currently existing. The regime, well versed in the art of remaining in power by eliminating alternatives and controlling the apparatus of coercion (rather than enhancing legitimacy and service delivery), has seen to that. Yet, non-political organisations can lend their support to political causes. Organised groups within China such as the Falun Gong, Roman Catholics (as opposed to Chinese Catholics) and independent trade unions are given close attention and are subject to significant persecution and control. The Chinese are well aware that there was the same confidence expressed in the viability of Communist regimes prior to the recent revolutions in the Soviet Union, Czechoslovakia, and Romania. For good reason, authoritarian regimes tend to take the possibility of revolution much more seriously.

Moreover, the regime is well aware that popular dissatisfaction with their lives by hundreds of millions, official corruption, and an inability to procure redress for injustices and frustrations has led to rising unrest and disenchantment with the Party. Furthermore, as more economic, administrative and coercive power moves into the hands of local rather than central officials, effective 'governance' by the vanguard of the regime becomes less feasible. The inability (and political unwillingness) to genuinely target the corruption problem is a prime illustration. The structural flaws and economic difficulties that lie ahead will exacerbate these conditions. How the regime responds is critically important.

(d) It only takes one spark …

A spark from heaven can light up an entire plain.

Deng Xiaoping

Winston Churchill once observed that great events in history rarely have great causes but are instead set off by the most minor of incidents, such as the assassination of an Archduke in Serbia as the trigger for the First World War. Those waiting for great causes to emerge generally miss the boat and there is more practical wisdom in seeking the conditions for great upheavals rather than specific grand causes.

Deng was certainly correct—when conditions pile up like bonfires waiting to be lit, it only takes one spark. There are a whole host of trigger events that cause unrest (having grown tenfold since 1993, according to official figures that are certainly conservative). Any of these hundreds of incidents each day—with the average size of them continually growing—are potential candidates that can constitute a 'spark'. If the beating of one migrant worker can cause 50,000 people in Chongqing to riot, and this is not atypical, then there are clearly deep rivers of discontent that incidents can tap into.

The regime's great fear is that rather than instances of social unrest being selectively isolated and reactive events, protestors will unite under common causes, with unrest becoming more organised and coordinated across different townships and even provinces. A few thousand peasants protesting about polluted drinking water in a small Western township is a very different proposition to the uniting of intellectuals, students and urban workers marching toward Tiananmen Square demanding greater political reform and protesting against CCP corruption (while eliciting widespread sympathy from the population for doing so.) Tiananmen remains the model of discontent that the regime is desperate to avoid.

Communication has always been the enemy of authoritarian regimes—especially those suffering profound credibility problems. Party officials are well aware that there are almost 450 million mobile phone users and well over 100 million Internet users in China. Sharing stories, incidents and ideas among themselves is an inherently threatening activity for the CCP. Although there is nothing inevitable linking the growing communication network and the rise of democracy or popular participation in China (despite what optimistic democratisation enthusiasts might argue), it is a new and profound challenge for the regime. Where once controlling the media, the spread of information and content was easy, it is now impossible. Populations that knew little about what was happening in the next town (let alone the next province) are now much better informed. The spread of facts and opinions, and also of completely unfounded rumours, increases every day. While watching CNN on Chinese satellite television is still a disjointed experience as snippets are regularly excluded or cut short, Internet savvy users can evade officially censored sites relatively easily and find out what they have missed from other sources. In one widely reported incident in October 2004, word of a simple traffic dispute spread so quickly that thousands of Hui from other parts of China learned of the clashes by telephone and rushed to the region before riot police could respond. A week later, a simple altercation between a deliveryman and a fruit market worker in western Chongqing attracted a crowd of thousands within hours via phones and text messages because the worker passed himself off as a government official and attempted to resolve the dispute in his favour. The protestors were making a point against someone they thought was a CCP official. Censorship in any form is simply much less effective in the age of modern communications.

Worryingly for the regime, the population is gaining knowledge about country-wide trends and statistics. A recent United Nations Development Program (UNDP) survey within China reported that 80% of Chinese believe that China's current income distribution is either 'not so equitable' or 'very inequitable'.[14] Most of those surveyed would have been educated urbanites who are far removed from the poorest in China. Moreover, where once books like the one written in 2004 by husband and wife team Chen Guidi and Wu Chuntao—*The Chinese Peasant Study*— would have been confined to foreign readership a world away, the banning of it has not prevented the estimated distribution of up to ten million copies through the underground press, making it a best seller. Millions of Chinese are reading passages from *The Chinese Peasant Study* like these:

> We observed unimaginable poverty and unthinkable evil, we saw unimaginable suffering and unthinkable helplessness, unimagined resistance with incompre-hensible silence, and have been moved beyond imagination by unbelievable tragedy ...

> Farmers worked all year long to earn an average annual income of 700 yuan (average annual urban income is 6000 yuan) ... There were 620 households in the

whole village, of which 514, or 83 percent, were below the poverty line. Even though the village was very poor, the leaders were prone to boasting and exaggeration about their performance, and as a result the government struck it off the list of impoverished villages. So the villagers were burdened with exorbitant taxes and levies.

Nor have the authorities been successful in stopping excerpts of the book being widely distributed through the Internet. The fact that the 460 page book can be easily bought under the counter for a couple of dollars throughout Chinese bookshops means that there are large segments of the population that are hungrily consuming information about the plight of their countrymen. The fact, also, that Chen is a member of the respected, state-sanctioned Association of Chinese Writers and far from a 'radical splittist', highlights the fact that it is not just outsiders who are shaking their heads at what is occurring in China. Indeed, commentary about the plight of the majority of Chinese and the root causes are occasionally taken up by factions within state sanctioned media, as well as state backed academics and intellectuals. While they rarely flirt with the great ideological and treasonous sin of 'splittism' (denouncing the Party as the legitimate rulers), it shows opening and festering wounds within the Party itself and concern about the plight of the people they lead.

What about urban elites? A recent Pew report appeared to offer a picture of optimism in which 75% of the predominantly elite urban respondents were generally optimistic about China's future.[15] This is not surprising as elites sharing disproportionately in a country's wealth tend to be optimistic. However, what this survey reaffirms is that China's elites have high expectations not just about China's economic growth but also expectations about continuing to benefit from this growth. While most instances of unrest have been in the countryside, urban movements tend to focus on loss of employment and non-provision of promised or accumulated social benefits such as pensions, health care, affordable housing and education.[16] (The primary triggers for the lost social benefits tend to involve officials embezzling or incompetently managing funds.) We have already seen that unemployment is increasing in both urban and rural areas as accumulated flaws begin to materialise. Pension funds, in particular, have been squandered and out-of-pocket expenses for healthcare have been increasing for a decade. It is doubtful whether such optimism in the urban regions is well placed.

Finally, the 'dark horse' of discontent is the *mingong*, the more than 200 million migrant peasant workers roaming mainly around urban China looking for work. These itinerant workers do not mix well with the elites, as one report describes:

> You can spot a *mingong* from miles away. Their work clothes, blue or brown, are shabby and covered in dust; they are thinner than most Chinese; and they are also shorter … Their armies can be seen in countless construction sites in Shanghai and Beijing, living in shelters more crowded than prisons cells … In this Beijing winter, late at night, they can be seen working in the streets under freezing temperatures and merciless winds from the Gobi Desert. Sometimes during a lightning-quick break one can spot their shadows gazing longingly at out-of-reach sneakers and mobile phones behind glittering department-store windows.[17]

The *mingong* constitute significant pockets of discontent in urban areas. About 25% never get paid or have their pay delayed by employers, 97% have no medical benefits whatsoever, and standards for work conditions are non-existent. To appreciate the scale of this kind of displacement, there are more *mingong* in China's biggest cities than there are registered urban workers.

No one can be sure where this is all leading. What I am arguing is that a China successfully in transition is far from the reality. We have seen that evidence reveals a regime trapped by its own contradictions. On the one hand, the extent of misallocated resources and dysfunctional macro-economic setup means that China's 'growth' economy cannot fulfil the regime's economic and social needs. Employment creation is falling dramatically short and social funds such as promised and accumulated pensions will not be there for millions when they need it. This is particularly worrying given China's well reported ageing problem. Moreover, the bursting of the bubble economy and the consequences of it are unpredictable but will certainly lead to massive social disruption. Even a slight tremor in the US economy would be devastating for China's growth economy which is so dependent on exports to America. Already, surplus rural workers are estimated at anywhere between 200–450 million while TVEs are declining and have already absorbed all the employees they can handle. Half of the rural migrants to the cities cannot find jobs. Bear in mind that the whole Chinese private sector only employs 200 million people. The unemployment problem is immense.

On the other hand, reform of the economy, including allowing private enterprises (who are best able to create and provide sustainable employment and consumption-led growth) access to key sectors and the majority share of capital, is needed. As the previous chapter argues, the regime is unlikely to allow this as its control of the most important levers in the economy would be unacceptably diminished. Moreover, such structural reform would cause the unemployment and displacement of millions of state workers and employees in state supported sectors. We would only have to look at the period from 1997–2000 when instances of civil unrest increased 235%. A high proportion of these instances were in urban areas experiencing accelerated lay-offs of SOE workers at a time when the leadership was looking to reduce the number of SOEs. The leadership is especially fearful of urban unrest as it would occur in the vicinity and in full view of China's elites and intellectuals, as well as the world's media.

Grass root level problems and the discontentment highlighted earlier—frequently flaring up unpredictably—are really just individual illustrations of the broader conditions in China made worse by interaction with corrupt officials. The possibility of regime collapse as a result of accumulated social deficits and declining legitimacy is dismissed by many in the West but not so by the senior leadership. President Hu repeatedly warns that a disconnect with the masses is the Party's greatest problem. In a Central Committee report in September 2004, officials were urged to improve governance amid the warning that 'the life and death of the party is at stake.' In a follow up article the next month, printed on the front page of the *People's Daily*, Vice

President Zeng Qinghong wrote:

> The Soviet union used to be the world's number one
> socialist country, but overnight the country broke up and
> political power collapsed ... One important reason was
> that in their long time in power, their system of governing
> became rigid, their ability to govern declined, people were
> dissatisfied with what the officials accomplished, and the
> officials became seriously isolated from the masses.[18]

Zeng might have been talking about the Soviet Union but
he has portentously listed the condition precedents for regime
implosion that exist in China now. Moreover, there is little
evidence the leadership has a plan to turn the tide and relies only
on tactical initiatives to put out 'spot fires', placate protestors or
else intimidate them.

(e) The dangers of managing disorder

Managing rising disorder is a dangerous activity. The important
and pertinent question is how the Party will respond as economic
and structural problems deepen, causing growth to slow, while
government and social deficits keep mounting. In other words,
how will the regime respond as instances of unrest multiply, and
the size and organisation behind them becomes more alarming?

As its mandate based on 'economic and social order
competence' fails, Dr Murray Tanner, an expert studying Chinese
unrest, observes that the basic strategy of the regime for retaining
effective power depends on 'driving a wedge of prosperity and
coercion between the enormous mainstream of average citizens
and the minority who might try to organise opposition [or]
promote systemic political change.'[19] Most importantly, this
means convincing the urban elites that the CCP can provide
them with continued economic growth, effective governance
and national unity and even national dignity. I have already
argued that the impetus of this strategy is stalling. Moreover,
the evidence of a more assertive mass political culture of protest
is compelling. The capacity of the regime to deliver is highly
questionable while there is a growing consciousness about
China's rural plight. This growing consciousness might very well

evolve into collective concern and anger should the situation of the economic elites deteriorate.

Second, the regime has two *tactical* ploys in attempting to manage unrest and discontent. The first is to deflect blame onto local officials rather than on the central government. The leadership encourages protestors to believe that the injustices they suffer as a result of actions taken by local officials are not typical of other regions or of the system as a whole, and that the central leadership would solve them if they knew. Unfortunately for the regime, this tactic is wearing thin as conditions worsen, grievances and petitions through formal channels are ignored, and information and stories spread via modern communication mediums.

Furthermore, the regime depends on the tactical use of permissiveness and repression, and compromise and coercion on a case by case basis. Manuals are produced for local enforcement stipulating principles and procedures with the aim of preventing unrest from escalating into major events. The problem with relying on this tactic is that it assumes a much greater level of professionalism and discipline from local enforcement authorities (who are usually the first onto the scene) than actually exists. The professionalism of these authorities, unsurprisingly, varies greatly from township to township. Moreover, as Dr Tanner observes, local police forces are often forced to serve two masters since the priorities and procedures of the central leadership often differ from those of local Party leaders.[20] Besides, when the corruption of local authorities is often the very issue driving the discontentment, it is implausible to always expect these same officials to respond calmly according to textbook procedures.

(f) Are there 'Tiananmens' looming on the horizon?

Assessing the prospects of future Tiananmen type incidents is not a preoccupation of China pessimists and policy hawks in Washington waiting for the country to stumble but an obsession of the CCP senior leadership. The pre-conditions for such incidents occurring again are clearly there. Should protestors unite and descend upon Beijing or Shanghai again, the important question is what the leadership will do—and seeing what they learnt (or did not learn) from Tiananmen in 1989.

There have been internal Party calls to revise the official interpretation of Tiananmen—as a treasonous 'counter-revolutionary rebellion' that was met with appropriate force by the authorities—which have been ignored by the senior leadership. Such revisions of official history are not just academic since they are expressions of official CCP policy which serve to guide future responses.

Bear in mind that the protests in Tiananmen were not calls for regime change but merely greater, albeit far-reaching, reforms. However, from the point of view of Deng, the authority of the CCP was being challenged in full view of the world's media. That in itself was sufficient for a 'tipping point' (although only after anxiously wrestling with the decision).

The first insight of Tiananmen is that the regime finds perspective and proportionality difficult to assess when it (and not just local authorities) is directly challenged. The second is that the massacre took place amid CCP indecision and chaos at the highest levels.[21] When push comes to shove and the leadership is placed under severe pressure, habits formed over five decades of authoritarian rule suggest that Party factions favouring coercion over compromise will endure. The CCP remains the unbending oak tree, not the reed. Challenges are viewed as a test of their 'resolve' or 'authority' that must be overcome as a 'matter of principle'. Unlike human rights advocates who primarily emphasise the dignity of the individual, hardliners in the Party core take the perhaps sincerely held view that preserving the authority and 'face' of the regime is the same as upholding China's collective dignity. Denigrating the Party through 'counter revolutionary' actions would fracture the history and principles of the 1949 revolution when China as a nation under one strong rule finally 'stood up'.

Tiananmen showed that brutal suppression can force protestors to abandon their demands for some time at least. It also shows that protest movements are capable of drawing support across many cities and provinces, even if the goals of different centres of protest were different. Since then levels of disaffection have become more profound and widespread than in 1989. There is increasing evidence that coercive tactics are backfiring and the use of force has actually increased calls by protest organisers to widen the scale of unrest against authorities. A further worrying sign for the regime is the rising numbers of prolonged protests that have lasted several months—another sign of declining authority and rising fearlessness (or desperation) of the people.

The regime's response: the emergence of the 'New Left' in Chinese politics

The preceding section provides the domestic setting that confronts President Hu. It is a China that Westerners rarely hear about or see. Yet, it is becoming the dominant issue in Chinese politics. Social turmoil rather than the need for further reform is increasingly influencing the regime's political agenda.

(a) The two faces of President Hu and the regime

As the unchallenged leader within the CCP, President Hu has two very different personas. The first is the one specifically designed for international audiences and is the one that successive Presidents since Deng have promoted outside China: the pragmatic 'reformer'. This is the image Hu pushed aggressively prior to his 2006 US visit and the one that captivated Australia in 2003. As Hu told the National People's Congress shortly before the US visit, his administration would 'uphold [China's] reformist orientation without hesitation' while official media ran stories about how government departments were set to 'storm the fortress' of reform. This was echoed by Premier Wen who announced that it is during the 11th Five Year Plan (2006–2010) that reform would enter the 'deep water zone'.[22]

The second persona is the one that is driven by domestic politics and rarely translated for a Western audience. As Jane Macartney wrote in *The Times* prior to President Hu's visit to the UK in 2005:

> He cultivates an image of humility and frugality. His first act in office was to drink tea with peasants ... But after three years in office his is a political record that has dashed early hopes he may be a great reformer

... He is a hardline communist of the old school on social policy. Behind the genial smile that will be on display at next week's Buckingham Palace banquet, and at the opening of the Royal Academy's *Three Emperors* exhibition, is a man determined to maintain the Communist Party's rigid control. He is a Brezhnev rather than a Gorbachev.[23]

What is behind the 'New Left'? Is President Hu indeed more a Brezhnev rather than a Gorbachev? Certainly, for senior leaders within the regime, the Soviet Union imploded not because the empire was in economic decline over two decades under Brezhnev but because Gorbachev was too radical and rapid in his reform attempts. Like most authoritarian regimes, the CCP prefers to be like the oak trees that stand strong against winds of change and resistance rather than reeds that sway and bend. Survival is seen as a matter of tightening one's grip, not relaxing it; retaining control of different levers of power, and silencing or isolating dissent rather than accommodating it. In other words, survival is seen to depend on strengthening the power and reach of the Party and, by their reckoning, the Chinese state.

Within a month of becoming the undisputed paramount leader (when he replaced Jiang Zemin as Chairman of the Central Military Commission (CMC)), Hu introduced Resolutions passed by the Central Committee that declared the foremost task to be the 'long reign and perennial stability of CCP rule' by 'strengthening the construction of the Party's governance ability.' For example, the Party needed to 'strengthen leadership over legislation work' and play a greater part in people's congresses, all levels of administration, and consultative conferences. Despite talk about 'multi-party cooperation' and 'consultation sessions', with China's eight so-called democratic parties, these parties are controlled by the CCP's United Front Department and are dependent on state financial support for survival. The solution to society's problems and complaints was therefore to be met by more extensive CCP power, not less.

It is important to understand that the CCP like other political parties is replete with factions: conservatives or leftists, liberals, reformists, nationalists, the Shanghai clique, Maoists, those with provincial interests and so on. Different factions blame each other for the social deficits that are building up in the country and the Party's unpopularity. Although Hu is the paramount leader, there is a constant need to consolidate his support within the Party. How is Hu trying to enhance his own status within the Party and the CCP trying to strengthen its power within China? The previous chapters looked at the CCP maintaining its hold on important economic levers and sectors as well as its concerted attempts to co-opt new elites. In addition to this, there are strong signals indicating the emergence of a 'New Left' with Hu at the helm that is intended to reinvigorate and strengthen the Party (and Hu's position) from within.

Former President Jiang attempted to sum up his vision with a rather obtuse 'Theory of the Three Represents' (that the Party represents the most advanced production forces, the foremost culture and the overall interests of the masses). In light of growing dissatisfaction, Hu consider this too elitist and slanted too much toward the empowerment of the new 'red capitalists' and put forward his own 'Theory of the Three Harmonies'. This triple harmony consisted of seeking peace in the world, 'reconciliation' with Taiwan, and harmony in Chinese society. While it is tempting to dismiss the Three Harmonies as gibberish, it does give us clues about Hu's orientation.

To reinvent purpose and reclaim unity, the classic authoritarian strategy is to emphasise the foreign demons poised and ready to enter into the kingdom. It is clear that Hu is falling for the temptation to use external influences as an internally binding force for the sake of his 'harmonious' China. The path away from political reform was made easier by the ailing health and eventual death of former CCP Chief Zhao Ziyang who died in early 2005. Zhao had been under house arrest since 1989. The image of Zhao tearfully begging the protesters at Tiananmen Square to stand down or be crushed by the impending arrival of army tanks remained a powerful image for many pro-reform Chinese. Prior to this, Hu who was actually once seen as more liberal then his predecessor, was already speaking about assassins in the shadows. The senior leadership from 2005 onwards had begun to decry forms of collusion between 'hostile foreign forces' on the one hand and 'bourgeois-liberal intellectuals' on the other.

CCP campaigns pushing for more social and economic reform were blamed on 'right wing' intellectuals and exponents of a traitorous 'new liberalism'.[24] There has therefore been moves in the last two years to weed out recalcitrant 'liberalists' or 'Western sympathisers', and a 'New Left' return to promoting 'Marxist rectitude' and 'ideological purity' among party members. Campaigns have been officially launched to re-educate the 70 million or so CCP members in Maoist, Marxist and Leninist thought to resist Western ideas about social and political reform. As one professor in the Central Party School pointed out without sarcasm, the campaign is aimed at building 'an ideological Great Wall' to safeguard the purity of cadres and party members. The aim was to develop the correct 'worldview, personal philosophy and value system' of party members.[25]

(b) Why the 'New Left' turn?

What is the psychology and strategy behind this leftward turn? Most commentators would put it down to Hu and his faction trying to consolidate their power. This is certainly true. Chinese politics, from senior leaders to local cadres, tends to split vertically down factional lines. By seizing the ideological agenda and appealing to the traditions of Mao and the thought of Marx and Lenin, Hu distinguished himself from his predecessor, Jiang, and reaffirmed himself as the champion of communism within the Party—a creed the CCP has never given up. By alienating the liberals, Hu is protecting the authoritarian regime from internal factions that seek more power sharing. Moreover, by returning to ideological purity, Hu is better able to deflect criticisms about slow or non-existent economic and political reforms.

Second, the 'New Left' is an attempt at recapturing the hearts of the hundreds of millions of Chinese who have not benefited from China's new wealth. It is a reaffirmation that the CCP is the Party of the masses. Hu realises that selling China's 'economic miracle' to those hundreds of millions of Chinese who have been left behind by the new middle class is an impossible task. Reconnecting with the masses, an objective wisely elevated by Hu as an urgent priority for the regime, means in practice an appeal to the concept of a continuing Socialist revolution in order to re-establish the primacy and irrefutability of the CCP's 'mandate from heaven'.

Third, this 'New Left' turn also bulks up Hu's PLA support base. Unlike previous leaders like Deng, Hu has had no military experience and has only very recently emerged out of the shadow of Jiang who had been the CMC Chief for almost 15 years before handing over to Hu. It was important for Hu to establish his credibility as the commander-in-chief, and the left turn—a move toward traditional revolutionary and ideological fervour, and away from liberal and capitalist philosophy—is generally welcomed by the PLA. Remember that the PLA is still the powerful embodiment of revolutionary nationalism in China. President Hu's elevation of the sons of First and Second Generation revolutionaries to senior PLA posts is the President indicating to the PLA that the revolution is ongoing.[26]

Finally, the 'New Left' is not just about an internal grab and consolidation of power. I mentioned that the Party is a paranoid regime fearful of both internal and external threats. With respect to external threats, despite consistent efforts to court the West, Hu sees interaction with the West and the US in particular as fraught with danger. For example, the CCP Leading Group on Foreign Affairs (LGFA), which is headed by Hu, closely watched the re-run of the presidential polls in Ukraine between the pro-West Viktor Yushchenko and pro-Russian Prime Minister Viktor Yanukovych. Despite differences between Hu and Russian President Putin, Hu agreed with Moscow's assessment that Yushchenko's victory was due to heavy support from 'Western interests' led by the US. In internal sessions devoted to the Ukraine elections, Hu's aides in the LGFA alerted the President to the belief that 'the West, led by the US, has been successful in infiltrating former Communist countries, thus resulting in their tilt toward America.'[27]

The LGFA subsequently raised the issue of a 'domino effect' in which Western-backed interests could emerge in former Soviet-bloc countries, including member countries of the 'Shanghai Cooperation Organisation' such as Uzbekistan, Tajikistan and Kyrgyzstan, which Beijing had made such strong efforts to court. Indeed, Hu made this explicit in an editorial in the *People's Daily* in January 2005 which claimed that 'hostile foreign forces have not abandoned their conspiracy and tactics to Westernise China and to divide up the country.'[28] The wealthy and increasingly urbane elites in China would be a prime target for these 'bourgeois' ideals.

New elites need to retain the faith. Pertinent to this has been Hu's criticism of former Soviet leader Gorbachev for introducing radical, Western style reforms to the 'detriment' of the Soviet Empire as well as his praise of regimes in Cuba and North Korea for successfully shielding their people from the subversion and infiltration of the West.

There is no doubt that Chinese leaders remain paranoid about 'colour revolutions' (for example, Ukraine's Orange Revolution and Georgia's Velvet Revolution) and 'democratic viruses' infecting potential breakaway provinces (such as Xinjiang) and eventually the whole of China. Hu's intensification of the crackdown on liberal intellectuals and continued oppression of organised groups like the Falun Gong, which might facilitate large democratic movements, must be understood in this light. Although there are no plans to return to any Mao-like isolationism from the (Western) world, China's deepening paranoia about having to resist democratisation pressures hatched by a conspiracy between external and internal enemies is very much behind the championing of the political aspects of the Beijing Consensus. Externally, it is clear that China's 'live and let live' ethics in international relations is very much a defence against Western calls for greater democracy. Internally, in some kind of conceptual retreat into revolutionary nationalism, any dissent or dissatisfaction with CCP rule is seen as a betrayal of national purpose at the highest level. In the eyes of the senior leadership, the state and regime are one, and any resistance against the regime is still the most serious act of treason.

The power of the gun: CCP-PLA relations

> Every Communist must grasp the truth: Political power grows out of the barrel of a gun.[29]
>
> *Mao Tse-tung*

The evolution of the Party's relationship with the PLA is probably the most important factor in understanding the future direction of the regime's domestic and foreign policy. President Hu ultimately depends on the PLA's support. The regime ultimately depends on the PLA's loyalty. China's foreign policy must receive the PLA's backing. Almost 70 years after Mao's observation, political power in China still grows out of the barrel of a gun.

The relationship between the CCP and PLA is a complex one. Although nowhere in the Chinese Constitution does it say that the PLA should devote itself to preserving the Party's supremacy, the PLA has been the 'steel Great Wall' of the Communist Party and the Chinese people (and not the state) since the beginning of the Revolution. The triumphant founding ceremony at Tiananmen in October 1949 and the rule of the CCP came to stand for the renewed *dignity* of China. The PLA remained the army and protector of the CCP, and by implication the protector of the Chinese people and the guarantee of China's newfound strength, unity and national dignity. The PLA was at the centre of China's re-emergence as a nation in the world. It was never just a professional standing army that emerged after the formation of modern China. Even though there were moves to institutionalise the role of the PLA as a professional state army during Deng's reign (*guojiahua*), the PLA remains both the CCP's army as well as the ultimate guarantor of domestic order and obedience. Almost all observers agree that the PLA is not yet a 'state army' in the full sense of the term.

To understand the extent to which the PLA is still effectively the CCP's private army, we should first consider that in an institutional sense, the debate is an artificial one. The Party *is* the civilian government. Although legislation tends to stipulate that the PLA exists to serve the 'state', there is no doubt that the PLA remain committed to the unique responsibility of protecting the regime (rather than the state per se) and keeping it in power. This was emphatically reaffirmed by President Hu shortly after becoming Chairman of the CMC in September 2004 when he issued instructions to China's top military commanders that the foremost function of the PLA was to 'provide forceful guarantee to enable the party to consolidate its ruling-party status.'[30]

However, the PLA is far from a passive servant of the regime. Loyalty, especially of those controlling the gun, usually has a price. The PLA undoubtedly has an interest in maintaining the power and authority of the CCP. However, many modern analyses get it wrong by treating the PLA as an apolitical and passive entity that merely waits for a winner to arise out of internal CCP power struggles. Mao might have expressed the desire to ensure that 'the Party commands the gun and the gun must never command the Party', but the CCP-PLA relationship is certainly much more complex than this.

First, civilian or Party control of the PLA is only very weakly institutionalised at best.[31] Even though the CMC is in principle answerable to the Central Committee, in practice it is the key military decision-making body and has been so historically. President Hu is the Chairman of the CMC but the other seven members are all serving PLA Generals. Moreover, titles tend to reflect personal allegiances rather than the other way round. That is, arguably, the nature of authoritarian politics in which power is rarely institutionalised independent of the individual. If it were, such systems would be more constitutional than authoritarian.

Second, while the PLA remains the Party's army it still identifies strongly with being the 'Peoples' Army'. While the regime remains successful at conflating the Party, regime, state and society, there is no conflict. However, with the Party's declining legitimacy in the eyes of hundreds of millions, cracks have significantly widened between serving the Party and serving the people. This was brought out most tragically at Tiananmen in 1989 when the reluctant Generals eventually agreed to fire at their own people. Although the PLA ultimately sided with the regime, the army was strongly shaken by the resulting loss of support of large sections of the population and has worked hard since then (for example, assisting during natural crises) to win back the respect of the people. As the common Chinese saying goes 'soldiers are the fish and people are the water; without water the fish will die.' It is unclear what the PLA would do in the event of another Tiananmen if the credibility of the Party as the peoples' party continues to suffer. A corrupt Party whose modern 'socialist' credentials are seen to be questionable will find it more difficult to demand the support of the PLA during a crisis if the Party's intention is simply to hang on to power.

Furthermore, many aspects of China's transition and modernisation, and its new found capitalist wealth, do not sit well with the PLA. In particular, the worsening income and regional disparities do not play out well with the PLA.[32] In a strong sense, the army is actually more in touch with China's poor than the leadership. Hundreds of thousands of conscripts return to their villages each year and are not shielded from the despair of common people. The beliefs and lifestyle of soldiers remain much more loyal to the principles of the Communist Revolution than increasingly out of touch officials.

The army is often called upon to aid people during crises, and work and live alongside them, unlike many CCP officials. The point is that while the PLA remains the 'Party's army', the relationship is potentially strained whenever the Party is seen to move away from the people. In this sense, the PLA is an inherently 'conservative' institution in that there is a suspicion of any move away from traditional Chinese Socialist principles and a deep distrust of modernising 'Western influences'.

Small cliques of 'liberal' PLA thinkers have been generally sidelined from the mainstream. In 1993, two distinguished army veterans famously voiced fears about China's and the PLA's continued exposure to bourgeois and capitalist elements in Chinese society. They felt that this would result in soldiers being seduced by 'luxury and pleasure' and corrupted by 'money worship, hedonism and extreme individualism.'[33] Since then, exhortations to remain true to traditional principles are frequently issued by senior PLA members who seek to limit the exposure of the rank and file to the upwardly mobile 'capitalist' classes. It is becoming more difficult to 'command the gun' when the Party is merely clinging on to power and is no longer seen as the committed guardian of socialist political ideology and values.

Third, although the CCP in principle largely controls funding and the power of appointment within the PLA, the bargaining process between the two bodies is less one-sided than institutional structure might suggest. As the PLA modernises and acquires what Samuel Huntington puts forward as defining professional armies—expertise, corporateness and responsibility—the PLA also becomes more aware of itself as a distinct entity from the regime, and aware of its interests and worth to the CCP. This is a worrying development for the regime since this is essentially a trend away from the PLA being a party-army (but not necessarily a shift toward the PLA being a state-army). We can see this in the preparedness of PLA leaders to publicly comment about developments in Chinese politics, give their opinions on military budgets, and even express approval or disapproval of political appointees.[34] The successful anti-satellite missile test fired by the PLA in January 2007—a provocative gesture by the military—was done without consultation with the Chinese Foreign Ministry.[35]

The broader implication is worrying. While the CCP struggles with its declining legitimacy, the PLA—an entity that is actually better organised than the Party—becomes perhaps the most formidable interest group that the Party must manage, placate and co-opt. The PLA was relatively neglected during the first 20 years of reform. Increased on and off-record military budgets in recent times growing between 15–20% year on year—officially at about US$30 billion but estimated to be US$70–120 billion by the US—is therefore likely to be as much a consequence of a co-opting tactic as a strategy of external power projection. Importantly, as the regime loses further domestic credibility, the PLA's influence is likely to increase given that its support is needed by the regime to remain in control.

Finally, this need to retain the support of the PLA is another reason why further liberalisation and reform of the system be resisted. Hundreds of thousands of soldiers are employed by SOEs. The PLA will not look kindly upon slowing credit for inefficient SOEs: this will immediately exacerbate unemployment since many of these firms will fail. Beijing's plans to slash subsidies and reduce tariffs in key areas, to fulfil WTO obligations will allow 'foreign devils' to enrich themselves by giving them open access to the economy, will not sit well with the PLA whose rank and file are largely the poor. Genuine market reforms in the most important sectors will be difficult since the CCP cannot suddenly overturn decades of pro-Communist and anti-Western rhetoric without undermining their credibility with the PLA. Instead, the inefficient strategy of fiscal stimulus through 'policy lending' by banks seems set to continue.

Conclusion

Mere growth cannot solve Beijing's domestic and social problems just as it cannot solve the structural problems with its economy.

These social and political problems are not simply the transient problems of a country in transition but arise largely because of an authoritarian regime that desperately defends its power and privilege. Chinese social and political deficits are serious.

Deng Xiaoping's 'keep a low profile' strategy, which focuses on economic development rather than military strength and confrontation, underpins China's 'peaceful rise' thesis. Domestic politics and concerns have meant that national security and hard power projection is making a comeback. As recently as 2003, President Hu declared that Beijing must pay greater attention to foreign affairs to 'make good preparations before the rainstorm ... and be in a position to seize the initiative.'[36] Premier Wen pointed out in a meeting of the State Council that 'We must boost our consciousness about disasters and downturns ... and think about dangers in the midst of apparent safety.'[37] The following chapter looks at possible consequences of a new form of nationalism that has been encouraged by the regime to rebuild legitimacy and social cohesion under its suffering leadership.

CHAPTER TWO

Uniting Against 'Foreign Devils'—Will The
Nationalism Card be played?

Chapter 2
Uniting Against 'Foreign Devils'—
Will The Nationalism Card be played?

Introduction

Speculation that China will engage in bouts of military adventurism to distract from domestic problems arise periodically. Such speculation, sometimes phrased in terms of China playing the 'nationalism card', is usually glibly presented and supported by little hard evidence.

However, the question should not be discounted as it is an important and serious one. Chinese nationalism is proud and enduring, and the country is undergoing a difficult and painful transition. To the outside world, China's rise seems spectacular. Within China, it is turbulent and even tumultuous. Domestic politics and pressures are beginning to wield their influence on foreign policy. The forms of nationalism that are emerging as a result must be considered. Will the 'nationalism card' be played?

In fact, it is already being played by the regime. There is convincing evidence that appealing to more virulent forms of nationalism is increasingly being used to rebuild support for its leadership, to deflect blame away from itself for many of China's problems, and to increase the Party's appeal to the PLA. Indeed, strong trends already exist that will increase of the likelihood regime playing the 'nationalism card' in the form of a more assertive if not aggressive foreign policy. These trends will most likely strengthen if domestic conditions continue to deteriorate. China's 'peaceful rise', although not yet discounted, should be revisited.

Chinese nationalism and emerging chauvinism

Unlike many revolutionary regimes, the CCP has intentionally promoted the rise of the Party as a modern chapter in the unfolding history of the world's oldest civilisation. The linking of ancient with modern (communist) China is very much part of the Party's positioning of itself as the legitimate and natural ruler of contemporary China. As one commentator observed, when Standing Committee Member Li Ruihan undertook the 'most uncommunist of acts' in laying a wreath at the tomb of the Yellow Emperor who was the legendary progenitor of the Chinese people, the action 'was designed to link the CCP with China's past.'[1] Indeed, part of the rhetoric is that the CCP is uniquely placed to lead the return of China to its former dignity and status, and to end its humiliation of the past 150 years.

This modern mission exists alongside a strong vein of national identity within Chinese society. Despite China's traumatic history, the identity of particularly the dominant Han culture has survived intact, and actual and mythical histories of China as the great Middle Kingdom at the centre of culture, commerce and power in Asia endure. Although there is no advocacy of a strict return to the tributary system overseen by China during the Ming and Qing dynasties, this period of Chinese history is still venerated in China's official histories. Indeed, it is promoted as a desirable and benign alternative to Western colonialism and 'post-colonial' intervention. More than this, some have argued that China's current foreign policy aims constitute a modern reinterpretation of the tributary system albeit in a much more subtle and sophisticated way more in tune with present-day diplomacy. For example, it has been argued that China—via increasingly successful attempts to lead stabilisation initiatives and co-opt regional neighbours through free trade pacts and the like in return for respect and recognition as Asia's leader from neighbours—is simply recreating its imperial security system and environment in a modern guise.[2]

The point is that the Chinese (with the exception of a few provinces and a handful of ethnic minorities) have maintained an unbroken sense of cultural identity, national pride, and national and cultural confidence despite turmoil and defeat throughout their history. A prominent China expert, Suisheng Zhao, observed that Chinese political elites began to embrace modern nationalism only after China's disastrous defeat by British troops in the 1840–1842 Opium War. This war led to both the eventual disintegration of the Chinese empire and the loss of sovereignty to foreign powers. As Zhao argues, 'Almost all powerful Chinese leaders from the early twentieth century through today have shared a deep bitterness at this humiliation and have determined to restore China's pride and prestige, as well as its rightful place in the world.'[3] In other words, modern Chinese nationalism is very much rooted in the painful humiliation of national defeat at the hand of foreign powers and the profound desire to return China to its former greatness. A large part of the success of the regime from Mao's time onwards was to represent the CCP as the defender of Chinese identity and nation *against foreign threats and influences*. The representation of foreign threats, therefore, is about threats against Chinese dignity and place in the world in addition to physical threats to its territory. Reclaiming Taiwan, for example, is at least as much about wiping away China's past humiliations as it is about removing America's 'unsinkable aircraft carrier' from the region.

A strong sense of nationalism does not in itself presage a disruptive China in the region and can instead be a positive cohesive force. However, President's Hu's 'New Left', which taps into this extant nationalism and blames many of the domestic problems on foreign influences and actors, clearly indicates the emergence of a new *chauvinism* in Chinese political direction. It is not really surprising that taking this path would be an appealing tactic for China's leaders facing mounting dissatisfaction. It presents a ready-made tactic to deflect blame, unite Chinese against perceived foreign enemies, depict calls for political reform and democratisation as insidious foreign ideas, and further entrench the idea that the CCP remains the champion of restoring China's national dignity in the world. Moreover, it also demonstrates the regime's resolve to senior PLA leaders who tend to be suspicious of, and hawkish against, these same foreign threats and influences. Crucially, these trends become more likely, not less, should the domestic situation worsen for the CCP.

A prominent China watcher, Peter Gries, warned a decade ago that an emotionally popular nationalism empowered by 'victim narratives [was] beginning to influence the making of Chinese foreign policy.'[4] Although such narratives exist in every country to some extent, it is of greater concern when authoritarian governments encourage and nurture them for their own purposes. In such systems, the battle of ideas is limited. Therefore, society's ability to discriminate between myth and fact, question official history, and ridicule blatant absurdities is limited.

In Australia, official histories of white settlement and treatment of Aboriginals—although a national wound—are openly examined. In Japan, there are public debates about the Nanjing massacre and whether Japan has adequately faced up to this dark chapter of its past. In China, schoolbooks and official histories still ignore or gloss over the famines of the Great Leap Forward and praise Mao's communists (rather than the Americans and the two atomic bombs) for defeating the Japanese in 1945. The point is that in systems where the regime has a mortgage on historical interpretation, understanding current affairs and defining 'truth', government backed chauvinism painting 'foreign devils' and 'demons' at China's doorstep are immeasurably more troubling. The possibility of the regime in a future time having to fuel the fires of a chauvinism they help nurture in order to placate a restless and frustrated peoples is a distinct danger. Professors at Chinese universities report that students are far less interested in liberal democracy and much more nationalistic than they were a decade ago. They are also much more likely to agree with using force to deal with China's 'enemies'.[5] This is additionally of concern when viewed alongside a recent Pew Global Attitudes survey in which an overwhelming 95% of Chinese respondents viewed their growing military power as a 'Good Thing'.[6] Importantly, according to Ying Ma, who worked for the US congressional commission on China, Chinese nationalism is becoming focused against America. Many Chinese 'increasingly view America as a bully ... thwarting the rise of their country's international influence.'[7]

National pride is strong indication of a cohesive society. But chauvinistic nationalism is something more dangerous. To cite an earlier account of the potential dangers of this sentiment, a testimony by Dr Joshua Muldavin (who has about 18 years of field research experience, mainly in China) to the *U.S.-China Economic and Security Review Commission* is edifying:

> I was in Beijing in a car that hit a bicycle in the mid-1990s. We were surrounded by a crowd of about 200. They started rocking the car; the broke the windows. They threatened us. And the chants were about national pride and how we rich foreigners could go

knocking down a person there … We zipped away in our smashed up car. But what was a key moment for me was how clear the nationalistic aspects of response could be utilised at any given moment in a threatening way.[8]

Since then, displays of aggressive nationalism have included massive anti-US demonstrations following the accidental bombing of the Chinese Embassy in Belgrade in May 1999 (that most Chinese immediately assumed the bombing was deliberate), spontaneous eruption of nationalist sentiment following the collision between a US Navy EP-3 surveillance plane and a Chinese fighter jet over the South China Sea in April 2001 (in which the Chinese pilot killed was declared a 'martyr of the revolution' and praised as a heroic defender of the motherland[9]), the thousands protesting against Japan's wartime atrocities, as well as Japan's pledge to help defend Taiwan in the event of invasion in 2005, and even mass public outrage misdirected against the US when Beijing missed out on the Olympics in 2000 (as many Chinese were quickly convinced it had thwarted Beijing's bid). In 2005, an Internet posting in China attracted 20 million Chinese signatures opposing Japan's bid to join the UN Security Council.

Protests and demonstrations occur in many countries but rarely do such mass demonstrations protest the actions of *other* countries. Public sentiment is fickle and can easily change. Edward Friedman cautions that there is 'no public opinion in China, only public sentiment.'[10] We should therefore be careful about reading too much into these fickle sentiments. However, when such public sentiment is partly created and strongly encouraged by the authoritarian government for its own interests, and is generally in line with long-standing PLA opinion, it becomes something more. As noted China expert Zhao asks:

Pragmatic nationalism is an instrument that the CCP uses to bolster the population's faith in a troubled political system and to hold the country together during its period of rapid and turbulent transformation … The question remains, can Beijing keep this nationalism reined in, or will it begin to accelerate out of control?[11]

Taiwan—The rebellious province

As the regime struggles against growing domestic hardship and disorder, splits within the Party will certainly occur. These splits may be public or behind closed doors. No doubt the so-called 'Democratic Faction' within the CCP will find a louder voice. However, it is doubtful whether even sustained economic and social crises could propel the faction to power. Prominent liberals such as those led by Zhao Ziyang were purged from the senior levels after the Tiananmen massacre and have not regained their influence. Short of profound regime incapacity and disintegration, the influence of the PLA will increase as leaders work to shore up the army's all-important support. Importantly, the 'Democratic Faction' does not enjoy the support of the PLA; the latter will unlikely see democratisation as a solution to worsening woes. Instead, there will almost certainly be increasingly forceful and desperate appeals to nationalism and national unity by senior leaders. As I speculated above, the confluence of a growing chauvinistic nationalism with the increased influence of what remains an inherently conservative and hawkish PLA is a potentially volatile meeting of circumstances.[12]

It is important to realise that despite the rhetoric about China's 'peaceful rise', China remains the only major power dissatisfied with its territorial borders. China still claims sovereignty over the disputed territories of the Spratly Islands and claims the whole of the South China Sea as its 'historic waters'. Taiwan and the Diaoyu Islands are still unresolved and Tibet, although now under the control of the PRC, remains a sore point. A quick look at standard Chinese geography textbooks reveals the drawing of borders and territory out of step with those that are internationally accepted.

Taiwan as an issue has probably become the most potent vestry of nationalistic sentiment for the Chinese: the regime, the PLA and the people. Taiwan is both an affront and an immense symbolic threat to the regime. It stands as an 'alternative' China that is a prosperous and thriving democracy. Moreover, the continued de facto independence of Taiwan has come to represent the conspiracy of foreign powers and foreign devils (especially the US) that work to frustrate what the CCP and PLA see as China's legitimate ambitions as a great power. Back in 2001, Evan Feigenbaum, executive director at Harvard University's Asia-Pacific Security Initiative, observed that 'Taiwan remains the single issue to which

China continues to subjugate any broad conceptions of grand strategy and, indeed, virtually its entire national security strategy.'[13] Forcing Taiwan back into the fold has been made into an issue of 'national dignity', and for a regime which has staked a lot of its credibility on 'returning Taiwan to the Motherland', the loss of Taiwan would be a serious blow to the legitimacy of the Party in the eyes of the people and the PLA. Given that the regime is already suffering profound legitimacy problems within China, the stakes vis-à-vis the Taiwan issue are raised even more. The Taiwan question is an unusual one since Taiwan does not in itself pose a hard security threat to China. Beijing's fear is a 'loss' of territory that they presently do not actually control, and that this territory will be lost not by force but by fiat emanating from that territory. As Thomas Christensen puts it, 'The danger to the PRC is that Taiwan might eventually move from de facto independence to legal independence, thus posing an affront to Chinese nationalism and a danger to regime stability in Beijing.'[14]

In one sense, Taiwan possibly represents the sum of Chinese irrationality. Staking one's internal (and external) power projection and prestige on recapturing a territory that is neither an existential threat nor even presently under one's control, is a dangerous perversion of sound and prudent national interest. The problem is that having raised the political stakes over the issue—in the name of nationalism and for the sake of regime legitimacy which is otherwise in trouble—to such an elevated level, the pressure to remain unbending and ultimately secure an outright 'win' is immense. This makes managing any Straits crisis much more difficult for two reasons, even more so if China's domestic situation deteriorates.

First, the political and security culture would move closer to that of the PLA's, which is generally hawkish, intransigent, and favourable towards coercive or military 'solutions' over diplomatic ones. Senior PLA Generals have periodically and unilaterally (without going through bureaucratic channels) warned Taiwanese leaders that the consequences of pursuing independence would be dire.[15] This means that any attempt by Taiwanese leaders to redefine the status quo or the terms of engagement, even if they fall far short of actually declaring independence, will be viewed in a more extreme light rather than as the usual diplomatic manoeuvrings inherent in any disagreement. For example, in an analysis of crises over the past decade between China and Taiwan, Richard Bush argues that attempts by Taiwanese Presidents Lee Teng-hui and Chen Shui-bian to merely redefine what future relations between the two entities might mean was treated as the beginning of an independence play and therefore in principle a *casus belli* as far as the CCP was concerned.[16] As an illustration, Lee Teng-hui's use of the term 'state-to-state' negotiations in 1999 was far from the declaration of independence that Beijing instantly took it to mean and the subsequent patrolling of the Straits by the PLA Air Force was ordered with little measured or considered thought. Beijing also obviously ignored the fact that their intransigence in these matters made steering a middle course much more difficult for Taiwan.

Second, there is a danger the fires of rampant, indignant and chauvinistic Chinese nationalism over the Taiwan issue could drive a defining and forceful response in the event of future crises. In a 2004 survey of about 2000 Chinese, 97.4% of respondents opposed Taiwanese independence.[17] On the one hand, any leader who the people perceive as having been tricked or out-negotiated by Taiwan and its allies (that is, predominately the US) will further undermine their personal and the Party's legitimacy. On the other hand, any leader who 'puts one over' Taiwan and its allies will have enhanced his and the Party's image. In this case, stubborn and inflexible action appears less risky than restraint and flexibility. Stand over tactics, even if irresponsible, appear a more viable approach than the prospect of appearing weak and losing face over the issue. Having fuelled and facilitated public anger against certain countries, factional and personal competition between leaders would increase the temptation to outshine or discredit rivals by proposing 'strong' rather than 'weak' responses. This offers every prospect of tragic and unintended escalation.

The analysis has been brief for such an important question but Taiwan is simply presented as the scenario in which political opportunism, chauvinistic nationalism and regime desperation is most likely to conspire with potentially disastrous consequences. The same kind of speculation could be applied to China's territorial dispute with Japan over the Diaoyu Islands (and to a much lesser extent the disputes with several ASEAN members over islands in the South China Sea). With the Diaoyu Islands issue in particular, the path is cleared for China to portray Japan's stance on the issue as reflecting a refusal to acknowledge the affront to the Chinese nation between 1895 and 1945.[18] The more general point is that if 'national dignity' rather than sober calculations of national interest become the dominant force behind foreign policy decision-making and escalation, the peaceful resolution of any crisis becomes immeasurably less likely.

China's 'peaceful rise'—An untested proposition

'Peaceful rise' is a strategy, not an end game. The Chinese quickly learned that overt aggression would be counter-productive. ASEAN nations, despite their differences, were generally united against what they saw as Chinese aggression in the South China Sea. China's clumsy manoeuvres in the 1990s both provoked the attention of the US and Japan (the two mainstays of Chinese 'encirclement') and threatened to drive regional states closer to these two powers. China was no match—militarily—for the US, let alone the coalition of the US and the region. Moreover, China learnt quickly the power of softer diplomacy in terms of both winning friends (for example, refusing to devalue their currency during the Asian Financial Crisis and gaining the gratitude of the region for doing so) and influencing countries (for example, giving unconditional aid to the region, leading security dialogues and so on). Finally, economic development and leadership was seen as a much better strategy to increase power and prestige. The world was happy to welcome China into the global market and China needed a stable and peaceful region to build a primarily economic foundation as a great regional and global power. 'Peaceful rise' was the happy compromise but it has never been articulated as an end game in itself and should not be axiomatically assumed to be one.

The difficulty with any scenario planning for China is that although Beijing has been undertaking a process of transition since Deng's reforms, contemporary China is remarkably undeveloped in terms of institutionalising its decision-making processes. Its processes are hazy and personality still exercises an inordinate amount of influence. The point really is that if we assume both the continued rise of a chauvinistic nationalism and the deterioration of conditions for the Party and the people, an ambiguous and highly individualistic decision-making process especially during a crisis throws up real possibilities of a much more disruptive Chinese foreign policy.

Except for Taiwan, China at this time would be reluctant to risk any direct conflict with the US. Its military capability and projection is still far short of the United States. Instead, elements of any disruptive foreign policy will largely involve other aspects of 'comprehensive power' projection and acquisition—international prestige, strategic aid, cultural influence and regional leadership—to gain influence at the expense of America and its allies. Chinese moves into Africa, Southeast Asia and the Pacific are well underway. However, for the future, as CNN China expert, Willy Lam, observes:

> Seasoned analysts have pointed out that the current leadership had decided late [in 2006] to make a clean break with Deng's cautious axioms and instead embark on a path of high-profile force projection ... A new generation of generals and strategists within the PLA apparently believes that Beijing has more to gain by attaining a 'balance of terror' between China and the United States.[19]

Are such arguments unduly speculative and treacherously alarmist? There are reasons why this may not be the case.

First, Chinese strategists and 'think-tanks' are undoubtedly advocating a 'great power mentality' in foreign affairs.[20] Losing Taiwan would be a humiliating blow against China as a 'great power'. We should be modest about the extent to which we can 'manage' the Chinese response to the Taiwan question.

Second, the assumption of China's 'peaceful rise' or 'peaceful development' emanating primarily from within China is itself an untested proposition. It is remarkable that it is accepted without contest in many parts. The interlocking segments of the 'peaceful rise' thesis—that China will continue to rise as an economic power; that it seeks to smoothly and seamlessly slip into the regional and global status quo as it does so; and that it has or will remove the military solution from the table of still critical and unresolved disputes—can each be seriously questioned. Just as war and conflict is never inevitable, neither is peace. To uncritically accept China's 'smile diplomacy' at face value betrays both prudent political practices and principles developed over centuries of international relations, and discounts existing Chinese posturing and behaviour. Opening (some of) China's markets and entering the global economy has served the country enormously well. While there is no doubt that 'peaceful rise' presents a compelling logic with which to further economic growth, it is not the only objective. Power and security, prestige, national honour and dignity, and most important of all, regime preservation, encompass the other goals. More immediate political priorities can override policies that are conducive to long-term economic growth. China would not be the first, or the last, country to go down that path.

Third, China and Chinese society is in rapid transition. It is surely important to examine the disturbing aspects of Chinese polity and society—the resolute but dysfunctional authoritarian system, the rise of chauvinistic (alongside civic) nationalism, the deepening of economic, social and government deficits and so on—to try to understand the ways they might interact and play out. Given these challenges, and combined with the uncertainty of external events, to argue that China will be an impeccably behaved, prosperous and successfully governed great power in the future is clearly more the product of unsighted speculation and wishful thinking than evidence.

Finally, where China's nationalism will take it in the longer term is unclear. Many commentators such as Henry Kissinger proceed on the basis that China is not a threat to the existing order and its rise should be seen as a peaceful one; only Western provocation would make it otherwise.[21] But in the event of a politically unreformed country, the broader question beyond Taiwan is whether stubbornly authoritarian China (whether it is rising or declining) will happily 'integrate' into a liberal world order and the regional security structure that is dominated by democratic (and liberalising) powers. James Mann poses this question in his recent book *The China Fantasy*.[22] Robert Kagan cautions us on the illusion of 'managing' China, asking:

> But isn't it possible that China does not want to be integrated into a political and security system that it had no part in shaping and that conforms neither to its ambitions nor to its own autocratic and hierarchical principles of rule? Might not China, like all rising powers of the past, including the United States, want

to reshape the international system to suit its own purposes, commensurate with its new power, and to make the world safe for autocracy? Yes, the Chinese want the prosperity that comes from integration in the global economy, but might they believe, as the Japanese did a century ago, that the purpose of getting rich is not to join the international system but to change it?[23]

Kagan concludes:

We may not know the answers to these questions. But we need to understand that the nature of China's rise will be largely determined by the Chinese and not by us.[24]

Even sensible and well-received calls from former US Deputy Secretary of State and current World Bank President, Robert Zoellick, for China to be a 'responsible stakeholder' in the global system promises a difficult path ahead. Responsibly working with the US and other powers when it comes to 'win-win' economic integration and trade policy strategies is one thing. Agreeing on global issues such as the relationship between defining and upholding 'sovereignty' on the one hand, and the legitimacy of regimes based on adherence to (even minimal) democratic norms and so-called 'internationally recognised standards' on human rights on the other will prove far more problematic.[25] More generally, Beijing's willingness to accept American leadership of this global order (within which China is urged to be a 'responsible stakeholder') is far from certain.

The point is not to make ironclad predictions about China's future. No one can claim to know this; not the Chinese nor the rest of the world. However, many experts are suffering a well-intentioned but self-induced 'China blindness'. China's model and its failures, and the link between domestic developments and foreign consequences, should be closely examined rather than too easily passed over or praised.

Part B
CHAPTER THREE

Conclusion

Chapter 3
Conclusion

Former *Time* magazine World Editor, Joshua Ramo, who coined the term 'Beijing Consensus' quite intentionally links the domestic and external 'virtues' of the Chinese model which together form the basis for the 'new physics' of development. According to Ramo, China is driven by both 'a ruthless willingness to innovate (domestically)' and a 'strong belief in sovereignty and multilateralism'. The Chinese model offers both hope to developing countries by providing 'a more equitable paradigm of development', and a model that 'safeguards the peaceful environment needed to secure its prosperity'.

In a sense, aspects of the 'Beijing Consensus' have given a new twist and presented a new stratagem against ascendant liberal economic and political positions that are now under attack for a number of reasons. Following the Soviet collapse, the relationship between liberal values, democratic systems, 'limited government' under the rule of law, and open economies on one hand, and prosperity on the other was once again confidently reasserted. The rhetoric about the inevitable march of political liberalism and free market economics was at its most compelling. The confrontational language of administrations like those of Reagan in the US and Thatcher in Britain immediately prior to the Soviet collapse appeared to have been justified. Liberal values and democratic regimes were no longer just the desirable product of post-Enlightenment Western culture; they were seen to be indispensable and reinforcing complements to prosperous societies.

Asian models such as those from Taiwan, South Korea, Malaysia and Singapore provided only intermittent and piecemeal challenges to liberal logic. These countries might not have been as liberal and as democratically mature as Western counterparts but they were ultimately democratising and moving away from centrally planned and protected economies, albeit sometimes at snail's pace. The link between open markets and democratisation was not really severed by these examples. Moreover, although leaders such as former Malaysian Prime Minister Mahathir went on the front foot by vociferously defending the right of individual countries to define their own standards of human and individual rights, Malaysia was not significant enough in the global scheme of things to signal an alternative to a model that had won out over its adversary in a global Cold War. The Cold War had absorbed the attention of the best minds from both sides lasting decades. An effective rabble-rouser leading a small but successful state was never going to seriously threaten hard won liberal orthodoxy.

However, what leaders like Mahathir did represent was the beginning of post-Cold War resistance against Western ideological pre-eminence in general and US hegemony in particular, of which the emphasis on linking legitimate sovereignty with human rights and individual dignity was seen as a tool of the hegemon. Moreover, this perceived American hegemonic order intimately linked individual rights with free and open economies, both of which were seen to be mutually reinforcing. This provided an obvious basis for criticism of countries that failed the standard, a criticism made more intimidating as it was delivered with the backing of the world's sole superpower.

That illiberal regimes (and authors like Ramo) would eagerly welcome a model to rival the liberal one was helped by strategists and leaders in the West abandoning rule-of-thumb realist principles guiding the use of force that were, with some exceptions, generally ascendant during the Cold War. With the threat of global war subsiding, Western governments flirted with a new ethics of force deployment away from more guarded realist ones. These included the humanitarian intervention debates in the 1990s culminating in NATO's Kosovo action against the Serbs in 1999, as well as the most recent Iraq War in 2003 in which the logic of removing a dictatorship and establishing democracy played a strong part in both the strategic and political justification. Although invading Iraq was also the result of pre-emptive principles in which the construction of what constituted an imminent 'threat' was significantly enlarged after the 9/11 attacks, the decision to invade Iraq and the ongoing problems with replacing Saddam's regime with a stable 'democratic' one for many discredited the notion of building liberal and democratic regimes through the use of force and from without.

The US led action represented different follies to different groups. Realists from almost all camps (who certainly rejected the logic of regime change) viewed Saddam's then-believed weapons-of-mass-destruction as an insufficient threat to the US to justify a full-scale invasion. Those states and regimes sneering from the sidelines rejoiced at the limits of US military power and what it could achieve. Importantly, a diverse collection of regimes and groups who craved an alternative to, or at least a lessening of, US hegemony and dominance for varying reasons focused on the violation of Iraq's sovereignty as the point of attack against an increasingly confident if not arrogant superpower. For regimes and interests that either rejected the logic of liberal economics and politics championed by the US, or felt threatened by it, the Iraq action and aftermath is cited as compelling evidence that regimes and countries should be left alone to do as they please. Predictably, the loudest of these voices were regimes that felt most threatened by the 'neo-conservative' democratising agenda.

It is within this context that the Chinese model—preferring sovereignty and non-interference over individual human rights—suddenly stood up strong as a counter-model to the liberal one. Although advocating liberalism or liberal society is a very different thing to supporting the American penchant for spreading democracy abroad (by force if necessary), distinctions between different questions in which one is about desired ends and the other about viable means are not reliably made in political and public discourse. Indeed, such distinctions are often intentionally ignored in order to make broad ranging political points. Subsequently, whereas the US was until recently viewed as the defender of global order after the Soviet collapse, the deep irony confronting us now is that authoritarian China is increasingly seen as the global champion of state sovereignty and a praiseworthy counterpoint to a US that many accuse of seeking to rewrite the rules of engagement for international relations. In other words, China is increasingly seen as the new defender of realist prudence in the world—Ramo's champion for stability and new global order. The 'live and let live' philosophy of the 'Beijing Consensus', of China's 'New Security Concept' in Asia, stands opposed to what many would see as the destabilising American liberal agenda for the world.

This has all been a diplomatic boon for China and the 'Beijing Consensus'. As the US struggles to help establish viable democratic regimes in Afghanistan and Iraq, the confidence and strength of liberal voices criticising the Chinese mix of authoritarian politics and hybrid (planned and free-market) economics diminished. Supporters of the 'Beijing Consensus' and authoritarian-led systems drew strength from the deflating of the American democratisation project (in Afghanistan and Iraq). Beijing suddenly appeared prudent and Washington reckless. Beijing's lack of regard for individual rights within its own system became irrelevant or at least was overlooked by liberals distracted by the struggling Iraq project. Importantly, aggressively advocating liberal or democratic agendas now appeared to be a failing Western obsession backed by an ailing hegemon.

In fact, there are manifold perversions of logic at work here. First, America's perceived failure in Iraq is not a failure of liberalism but a failure to understand the dynamic of sectarian and ethnic rivalries deepened by decades of selective repression in a foreign land. In other words, it does not signify a failure of liberalism or its logic but the failure of an instance of American foreign policy. Second, the difficulty of establishing a workable democracy in Iraq should not confirm the virtue of, and strengthen the case for, authoritarian politics but merely be an argument against the viability of spreading democracy by force. Third, even if we accept China's self-serving championing of sovereignty and non-interference as the more prudent terms of international relations, the issue of China's authoritarian model is a different question altogether. Arguing against interventionism in the name of upholding national sovereignty is not the same as vindicating authoritarianism in the Chinese domestic system. China's model still has to be judged by its own lights unaided by perceived failures in US foreign policy.

The last point is all-important. One must ignore illogical temptations to distribute in equal measure criticism of the US and its foreign policy with praise of China's domestic and international model. The 'Beijing Consensus' must be judged by the evidence of what is occurring in China; whether the regime's poor enthusiasm for political reform and rejection of what it portrays as Western notions of 'individual dignity' and 'individual rights' presents a successful and plausible alternative to liberal and democratic models.

Proponents of the 'Beijing Consensus' and admirers of 'market socialism' variously argue that China is getting it right, and that we should remain patient and optimistic. I have argued that the economics and politics behind the Chinese model are flawed, unsustainable, dangerously unstable, and unlikely if not incapable of providing a foundation for the continuation of China's 'peaceful rise' or 'peaceful development'. China has not developed a new and successful logic of political-economy—a new physics of development and power—despite the hype. They have not found a new logic to supplant the claims of liberal systems which put forward links between freedoms enshrined in the political and economic order and sustainable economic prosperity. China's destiny is more in Chinese hands than we would like in the West. Taking this sober and solemn look at what lies behind 'market socialism' should be the first step to '*getting* China right'.

In a forceful and compelling essay examining the dialectic of nationalism and liberalism within Chinese society, John Fitzgerald argues that 'dignity' is the essential (albeit contested) concept that is common to discourses on individual rights and national prestige. Chinese nationalism has therefore inadvertently incubated an idea of human rights or 'individual dignity' in which 'resurgent nationalism ... offers ground for hope that China's wheel is turning, slowly but surely, to recognising the inherent dignity of the individual.'[1]

We cannot do justice to the depth of Fitzgerald's argument here but the essay introduces an important point. China's ambition is rooted deeply in its quest for recognition and a reversal of what it sees as its humiliation that lasted for generations. The world must come to grips with this politics of indignation or what Fitzgerald calls *nationalist ressentiment*. China must therefore be engaged, not shunned. But from this point, future paths diverge. Engaging China cannot presume that such engagement will lead to the inevitable and seamless democratisation and liberalisation of the country and society, that the renewed dignity of Chinese nationalism will converge with respect for the dignity of the individual. China remains an authoritarian and repressive polity. Remaining so is precisely what aspects of the 'Beijing Consensus' or 'market socialism' implies and applauds. Chinese authoritarian logic asserted that retaining such a system was needed to avoid disorder and guard against the mounting of social and governance deficits that would surely arise during any transition process. Yet, this logic has been shown to be flawed, contradictory and duplicitous. China's rulers are explicit in that they do not intend a transition that will ultimately reduce their power, role and reach. The regime's 'opening' up of China and engagement with the world is being done to entrench and salvage its own exclusive rule.

The logic and benefits of these freedoms (and restraints on government) are being denied to the country in the name of a model of politics and economics that is failing. Engagement must proceed with collective eyes that are wide open to these profound failings and contradictions, and not merely proceed on the basis of 'integrating' China as if it were a straight-forward matter of accommodating just one more large country into the existing security and economic space. The China question presents a moral challenge, not just a strategic one. In both moral and strategic realms, the challenge is far more subtle, oblique and sophisticated than the one the Soviet Union presented to the West. China does not seek to explicitly defeat the West but to legitimately take its place as one of the genuinely great powers. However, its regime seeks to do so armed with a moral and political reasoning that is at odds with the freedom and restraints on governments in the West.

The world wants China to succeed for economic, political and humanitarian reasons. The alternative would condemn over a billion Chinese to a grim existence. That China's current model is failing, not succeeding, makes the moral and strategic challenge more profound, not less. An uncertain and struggling giant state that is no less ambitious is a greater dilemma for the world than a confident and successful one in many ways.

Finally, our capacity to influence domestic developments within China is severely limited. Certainly, we should argue against and hope that the US does not capitulate to uninformed and short-sighted calls to follow the path of protectionism which would both embolden the sceptics of free trade and global engagement within China and cause considerable damage to Chinese development and its people. We can also caution against any reckless and ill-considered 'independence' moves by Taiwan's leaders. To be sure, we can mostly only watch from the sidelines as well as avoid outdated 'containment' strategies that provoke unnecessarily and are likely to be counter-productive. But it is similarly irresponsible to simply assume that the logic of economic globalisation, and China's increasing participation in the system, will somehow melt away outstanding and awkward political challenges as a result of China's re-emergence.

The primacy of economics over politics in the case of the 'China question' is far from certain. Ross Terrill argues that 'being wary of authoritarian China yet engaging with emerging China is a dualism we can and should live with.'[2] No matter the strategy, in 'engaging' China, we should be careful not to turn a blind eye to—much less support—a reasoning that stands tragically in contrast to the one that sustains our continued good fortune.

ENDNOTES

Introduction

[1] Andreas Lorenz and Wieland Wagner, 'Does Communism Work After All?', *Der Spiegel*, (27 February 2007).

[2] See Meghnad Desai, 'Debate: Does the future really belong to China?', *Prospect Magazine* (January 2007).

[3] See Albert Keidel, 'Why China Won't Slow Down,' *Foreign Policy* (May/June 2006).

[4] C. Fred Bergsten, Bates Gill, Nicholas R. Lardy, & Derek Mitchell, *China: The Balance Sheet* (New York: Public Affairs, 2006), p 39.

[5] See Jason Potts, 'Evolutionary Economics' *Policy* 19:1 (Autumn, 2003), p 58-62.

[6] Robert Kagan, 'The illusion of "managing" China,' *Washington Post*, 15 May, 2005.

Chapter 1

[1] 'Milton Friedman @ Rest,' *The Wall Street Journal*, 22 January 2007, p A15.

[2] Greg Sheridan, 'Chinese model passes the test', *The Australian*, 25 August 2005, p 23.

[3] Joshua Cooper Ramos, *The Beijing Consensus*, (London: The Foreign Policy Centre, London, 2004), p 3.

[4] Milton Osborne, *The paramount power: China & the Countries of Southeast Asia,* (Sydney: Lowy Institute for International Policy, 2006).

[5] Michael Novak, *The Spirit of Democratic Capitalism,* (New York: Simon and Schuster, 1982); *Free Persons and the Common Good,* (Lanham: Madison Books, 1989).

[6] Timothy Ash, 'Global capitalism now has no serious rivals. But it could destroy itself,' *The Guardian*, 22 February 22 2007.

[7] See Samuel P. Huntington, *Political Order in Changing Societies* (Yale University Press, 1968).

[8] Michael Novak, *The Catholic Ethic and the Spirit of Capitalism*, (New York: Simon & Schuster, 1982).

[9] Martin Wolf, 'Europeans can look to each other,' *The*

Financial Times, 13 September, 2005.

[10] Joshua Ramo, *The Beijing Consensus*.

[11] As above.

[12] Kishore Mahbubani, 'When Asia Emerges, How Will the World Change?', *AsiaViews*, 12 April 2004.

[13] Mark Leonard, 'The Road Obscured: New Left or Neo-Comm'?, *Financial Times*, July 9, 2005, p 32.

[14] Greg Sheridan, 'Chinese Model Passes the Test', p 23.

[15] Thomas L. Friedman, 'Thou Shalt Not Destroy the Center', *New York Times*, 11 November, 2005, p A23.

[16] See Robert Kagan, 'The illusion of 'managing' China', *The Washington Post*, 15 May, 2005, p B07.

[17] See Joshua Kurlantzick, 'How China is Changing Global Diplomacy', *New Republic*, 27 June 2005, p 17.

[18] As above.

[19] See Richard McGregor, 'China's success inspires envy and awe,' *The Financial Times*, May 28, 2004, p 8.

[20] See Moises Naim, 'Help not wanted,' *New York Times*, February 15, 2007

[21] See Department of Defence (DoD), *Australia's National Security, A Defence Update 2005*, (Canberra: DoD, 2005), p 6.

[22] Department of Foreign Affairs & Trade (DFAT), *Advancing the National Interest: Australia's Foreign Affairs and Trade Policy White Paper*, (Canberra: DFAT, 2003), p 79.

[23] As above

[24] See Kevin Rudd, *Australia's Engagement with Asia: A New Paradigm?*, AsiaLink ANU National Forum, 13 August, 2004; 'Australian and China: A Strong and Stable Partnership for the 21st Century,' Speech to The Central Party School of the Communist Party of China, Beijing, 1July, 2004.

[25] Quotes by Presidents Clinton and Bush cited in Ying Ma, 'China's Stubborn Anti-Democracy', *Policy Review* (February/March 2007).

Chapter 2

[1] See Paul Monk, *Thunder from the Silent Zone: Rethinking China*, (Sydney: Scribe, 2005).

[2] Thomas Rawski, 'The credibility gap: China's recent GDP statistics,' *China Economic Quarterly 5:1* 2001, p 18-22.

[3] Martin Wolf, 'Why is China growing so slowly?', *Foreign Policy*, January/February, 2005, p 1-2.

[4] When China's 'economic miracle' began in 1978, its GDP per capita was one twentieth of the US Japan's was one fifth of the US in 1950 even before Japan's surge began.

[5] 'Build Socialism with Chinese Characteristics', in Deng Xiaoping, *Selected Works of Deng Xiaoping Volume III 1982-1992* (San Francisco: Foreign Languages Press, 1994).

[6] See Deng Xiaoping, *Selected Works of Deng Xiaoping, Volume II 1975-1982*, (Beijing: Renmin, 1983), p 301.

[7] Minxin Pei, *China's Trapped Transition,* (London; Harvard University Press, London, 2006), p 47-8.

[8] As above, p 324.

[9] The duration of contracts was 15 years in the 1980s and extended to 30 years in 1993.

[10] See Shenggen Fan, 'Production and Productivity Growth in China Agriculture: New Measurement and Evidence,' *Food Policy* 22:3 (1997), p 213-28.

[11] See Kate Zhao, *How the Farmers Changed China* (CO: Westview Press, 1996).

[12] Quoted in Will Hutton, *The Writing on the Wall*, (London: Free Press 2007), p 99.

[13] OECD, *Governance in China: Fighting Corruption in China*, (Paris: OECD, 2005).

[14] Huang Yasheng, cited in 'Prosperity choked from above', *The Australian*, 26 August, 2006

[15] The term was first used by Barry Naughton, *Growing out of the plan*, (New York: Cambridge University Press, 1995).

[16] Minxin Pei, *China's Trapped Transition, p* 25.

[17] Speech by Jiang Zemin, general Secretary of the Central

Committee of the Communist party of China, at the Meeting celebrating the Eightieth Anniversary of the Founding of the CCP.

[18] See Charles Wolf, Jr., K.C. Yeh, Benjamin Zycher, Nicholas Eberstadt, Sung-Ho Lee, *Fault Lines in China's Economic Terrain*, (Santa Monica: RAND, 2003).

Chapter 3

[1] Gordon G. Change, *The Coming Collapse of China* (London: Arrow, 2002), p 221.

[2] For example, see the Corruption Perceptions Index 2005, http://www.transparency.org

[3] 'China's next revolution,' *The Economist*, 8 March 2007.

[4] As above.

[5] Simon Pritchard, 'Capitalism without bankruptcy', *South China Morning Post,* 31 October 2001.

[6] See Carsten A. Holz, 'Have China's Scholars All Been Bought?', *Far Eastern Economic Review*, April 2007.

[7] Morris Goldstein and Nicholas Lardy, 'What Kind of Landing for the Chinese Economy?', *Institute for International Economics* (Washington DC: IIE, 2004).

[8] These are taken from the National Bureau of Statistics of China website and are based on 2005 figures. See www.stats.gov.cn

[9] 'Special Report: China', *The Economist*, March 18, 2004.

[10] Ernst & Young, *Global Nonperforming Loan Report 2006*, (London: Ernst & Young, May 2006), p 15.

[11] Ibid., at 14. See also James T. Areddy, 'Ernst Illustrates Risk to Guessing China's Bad Debt,' *Wall Street Journal*, 16 May, 2006, p C4

[12] As above.

[13] Fitch Ratings, 'China: Taking Stock of Banking System NPLs,' 30 May 30, 2006: http://www.fitchratings.com/dtp/pdf2-06/bchi3005.pdf

[14] Standard & Poor, *Rapid Rise in Interest Rates or Renminbi Could Stretch China's Embryonic Banking System*, (New York:

S&P, 26 June 2006). S&P estimates that bad loans at the end of 2005 amounted to between US$520-620 billion.

[15] See Dai Xianglong, Governor of People's Bank of China in 1995, and Chairman of Bank of China's Monetary Policy Committee in 1997, cited in Yi Zhao (ed.), *The Formation and Handling of Nonperforming Assets in China's State Commercial Banks*, (Beijing: China Price Press, 2001), p 3.

[16] See *The Economist*, 14 February, 1998, p 37.

[17] Deutsche Bank Research, *China's financial sector*, (New York: Deutsche Bank, 9 January, 2004), p 10.

[18] *The Economist*, March 8, 1997, p S16.

[19] As above.

[20] For example, see comments by Fang Xinghai, the first head of a committee heading loan transfer between China Cinda Asset Management Corp (the first AMC) and China Construction Bank, 29 April 2002: http://www.chinadaily.com.cn

[21] Figures derived from Deutsche Bank. Deutsche Bank Research, *China's financial sector,* p 10.

[22] Fitch Ratings, 'China: Taking Stock of Banking System NPLs, p 3-4.

[23] For example, see *The Economist*, September 13, 1997, p 26.

[24] Gordon G. Chang, *The Coming Collapse of China*, p 124.

[25] For example, see comments by Fang Xinghai, the first head of a committee heading loan transfer between China Cinda Asset Management Corp (the first AMC) and China Construction Bank, 29 April 2002: http://www.chinadaily.com.cn

[26] *Moody's China Banking System Outlook* (Beijing: Moody's, October 2002).

[27] See http://www.CEICdata.com

[28] As above

[29] See Minxin Pei, *China's Trapped Transition*.

[30] Fan Gang, 'China's nonperforming loans and national comprehensive liability,' *Asian Economic Papers* 2:1 (2003), p 145-152.

[31] Paul Heytens & Harm Zebregs, 'How fast can China grow?', in *China – Competing in the global economy*, ed. Wanda Tseng and Markus Rodlauer, (New York: IMF, 2003).

[32] Stephen Roach, 'Scale and the Chinese Policy Challenge,' *Global Economic Forum* (New York: Morgan Stanley, 19 June, 2006).

[33] See Minxin Pei, 'How Rotten Politics Feeds a Bad Loan Crunch in China', *The Financial Times*, 7 May 2006, p 9.

[34] Andy Xie, 'Running out of room to stimulate', 3 January 2002: http://www.chinaonline.com; McKinsey & Co Global Institute, reproduced in Diana Farrell & Susan Lund, Putting China's Capital to Work (New York: Mckinsey Global Institute, 2006).

[35] See *The Economist*, 18 March, 2004. A report in 2002 by James Kynge suggested that in that period, 80 percent of manufactured products were in chronic oversupply: 'China's changing of the guard halts key reforms', *The Financial Times*, 7 September 2002, p 4.

[36] See Gordon Chang, *Statement to US-China Economic and Security Review Commission*, (Washington DC, 22 August, 2006).

[37] See http://www.pbc.gov.cn

[38] Charles Wolf Jr., K.C. Yeh, Benjamin Zycher, Nicholas Eberstadt, Sung-Ho Lee, *Fault Lines in China's Economic Terrain* (Santa Monica: RAND, 2004), p 127.

[39] See Nicholas Lardy, *China's Unfinished Economic Revolution* (Washington DC: Brookings Institute Press, 1998) on the new 'fiscal' role of the banks.

[40] See Nicholas Lardy, 'Op Ed: China's Worsening Debts", *The Financial Times*, 22 June 2001, p 13.

[41] *Quarterly Update, February 2006*, (Beijing: World Bank Office, 2006).

[42] See *Statistics of China's Industrial Economy, 1949-1984* (Beijing: China Statistics Press, 1985); *China Statistical Abstract, 2001* (Beijing: China Statistics Press, 2001).

[43] See Usha Haley, *Statement before the US-China Economic & Security Review* (Washington DC, April 4, 2006).

44 Haihan Zheng (ed.), *A Study of the Losses of State-Owned Enterprises*, (Beijing: Economic Management Press, 1998).

45 David Dollar and Shang-Hin Wei, *Das (Wasted) Kapital: Firm Ownership and Investment Efficiency in China* (Washington DC: IMF, January 2007).

46 Minxin Pei, *China's Trapped Transition*, p 31.

47 June 25, 2004: http://www.chinanews.com.cn

48 See *The Economist* (Mar 18, 2004).

49 See http://www.china.org.cn/baodao/english/newsandreport/2002december15/24-3.htm

50 Stephen Green, *Reforming China's Economy: A Rough Guide* (London: Royal Institute of International Affairs, 2003), p 14-5.

51 Gary Jefferson et al., 'Ownership, productivity change and financial performance in Chinese industry', *Journal of Comparative Economics* (28, 2000), p 786-813.

52 National Bureau of Statistics of China: http://www.stats.gov.cn/english

53 22 February 2003: See http://www.peopledaily.com.cn

54 See Alwyn Young, 'The Razor's Edge: Distortions and Incremental Reform in the People's Republic of China', *The Quarterly Journal of Economics* (115:4, 2000), p 1091-1035.

55 The automobile industry brings this out. Of the 116 Chinese manufacturing plants in 1996, average output was about 12,600 per plant but only 18 were making more than 10,000 each year. Furthermore, of ninety four major industrial categories, there was excess capacity in sixty one of them, and 35 of them had a capacity utilisation rate of under 50 percent. However, gross output numbers of the industry looked impressive, even though most individual firms were loss making. See Minxin Pei, *China's Trapped Transition*, p 128-9.

56 State Planning Commission, 'A Study on Local Protectionism in the Automobile Market and Policy Prescriptions', 2001; cited in Minxin Pei, *China's Trapped Transition*, p 127.

57 Cited in Gordon Chang, Testimony to US-China Economic

Security Review Commission (Washington DC, 2003).

58 For example, see OECD, *China in the World Economy: The Domestic Policy Challenges*, (Paris: OECD Publication Service, 2002).

59 See above, p 69.

60 See Sharif Shuja, 'The Limits of Chinese Economic Reform,' *China Brief,* (V:17:2, 2005), p 9.

61 *China Statistical Yearbook, 2004*, (Beijing, Government Press, 2005).

62 As above.

63 Jonathan Anderson, 'Five Persistent Myths About China's Banking System', *Cato Journal* (26:2, 2006), p 248.

64 See James Kynge, 'Creaking economy needs stronger foundations', *The Financial Times*, 30 October 202, p 5.

65 Taken from a speech delivered by Professor Lu Tong, Director of the Chinese Centre for Corporate Governance of the Institute of World Economics and Politics at the Chinese Academy of Social Sciences, to the Faculty of Commerce, University of Melbourne, 29 September 2006.

66 Figures according to Finance Minister Xiang: 'China To Continue Pro-Active Fiscal Policy: Finance Minister,' *People's Daily Online*, 17 April 2002.

67 National Bureau of Statistics of China: http://www.stats.com.cn

68 See 'More cold showers for China,' *Asia Times*, 20 June 2006: http://www.atimes.com/atimes/China_Business/HF20Cb05.html

69 People's Bank of China, *2003 China Monetary Policy Report* (Beijing: Government Press, 2004), p 13.

70 National Bureau of Statistics of China: http://www.stats.com.cn; See also *China Statistical Yearbook,* (Beijing: Government Press, 2003), p 316; *China Statistical Abstract* (Beijing: Government Press, 2004), p 50; 'NDRC: China's fixed asset growth may lead to over-heating', 3 August 2006: http://www.chinadaily.com.au; Xu Dashan, 'Fixed asset investment growth slowing', 14 June 2006: http://www.chinadaily.com.au

71 See Stephen Roach, 'Scale and the Chinese Policy Challenge.'

72 Cited in Minxin Pei, 'The Dark Side of China's Rise', *Foreign Policy* (March/April 2006), p 2.

73 Council for Economic Planning & Development, 1997, *Taiwan Statistical Data Book 1997*, (Taipei 1998).

74 People's Bank of China, *Report on the Implementation of Monetary Policy in 2004Q1*, Beijing: Government Press, 19 May 2004).

75 See *China Statistical Abstract 2004*.

76 Research cited in Morris Goldstein and Nicholas Lardy, 'What kind of landing for the Chinese Economy?', *Policy Brief* (Washington DC: Institute for International Economics, November 2004), p 6.

77 For example, see Jonathan Anderson, Chief Asian Economist, UBS, 'China's True Growth: No Myth or Miracle,' *Far Eastern Economic Review* (169:7, September 2006).

78 Paul Krugman, 'The Myth of Asia's Miracle,' *Foreign Affairs* (73:6, 1994), p 62-78.

79 See above. See also Alwyn Young, 'Tale of Two Cities: Factor Accumulation and Technical Change in Hong Kong & Singapore,' *NBER Economics Annua,* (1992), p 13-54.

80 See Paul Krugman, 'The Myth of Asia's Miracle', p 72.

81 See research by McKinsey & Co Global Institute, reproduced in Diana Farrell & Susan Lund, 'Putting China's Capital to Work,' *Far Eastern Economic Review*, 1 May, 2006.

82 See 'Prosperity choked from above', *The Australian*, 26 August, 2006.

83 Quoted in above.

84 Quoted in Huang Yasheng & Tarun Khanna, 'Can India overtake China?', *Foreign Policy* (July/August 2003).

85 Cited in Minxin Pei, 'The Dark Side of China's Rise', p 1.

86 There are other extremely serious risk factors such as environmental resource management and degradation that could trigger a widespread crisis throughout China but we will confine the paper to the economic and political factors already discussed.

[87]   See Michael Overmyer, 'WTO: Year Five', *China Business Review* (January/February 2006).

[88]   Gordon Chang, *The Coming Collapse of China*, p 6.

[89]   *People's Bank of China Statistics* (Beijing: Government Press, January 20, 2006).

[90]   Steven Solnick, 'The Breakdown of Hierarchies in the Soviet Union and China: A Neoinstitutionalist Perspective', *World Politics* (48:2, 1996), p 209-38.

[91]   This is reflected in the increasing current account surplus from US$17 billion in 2001, US$69 billion in 2004, and about US150 billion in 2005, almost 7 percent of GDP: see remarks by Timothy Adams, Treasury Under-Secretary for International Affairs to the Asia Society, April 7, 2006: http://www.asiasociety.org/speeches/06tx_adams.html

[92]   As a comparison, US per capita GDP in 2005 was $43,000, while per capita foreign trade was $11,196. Take away foreign trade and US per capita GDP would be $31,804: see Henry Liu, 'Part 2: The US-China Trade Imbalance,' *Asia Times*, 6 April 2006: http://www.atimes.com/atimes/China_Business/HD01Cb05.html

[93]   David Dollar, 'China's Economic Problems [and ours']', *The Milken Institute Review* (Third Quarter, 2005), p 50-1.

[94]   See G.J. Gilboy, 'The myth behind the Chinese miracle,' *Foreign Affairs* (83, 2004), p 33-48.

[95]   Nicholas Lardy, China: The Great New Economic Challenge?, *Institute for International Economics* (Washington DC: IIE, 2004), p 132-3.

[96]   'China's economic growth poses no threat', *Xinhua*, 22 January 2007: http://www.chinadaily.com.cn/china/2007-01/22/content_789623.htm

[97]   Huang Yasheng & Tarun Khanna, 'Can India overtake China?'

[98]   Paul Krugman, 'The Myth of Asia's Miracle', p 72.

[99]   Above, p 67.

[100]   See Scott Macdonald, 'Wen: China Democracy 100 years away,' *Time*, 27 February, 2007.

Chapter 4

[1] Taken from The Peking Duck blog site, July 6, 2006: http://www.pekingduck.org/pond//viewtopic.php?t=431

[2] *China Statistical Abstract 2000*, at 84.

[3] See research by Minxin Pei, *China's Trapped Transition*, p 192-4.

[4] See Charles Wolf Jr., et al, *Fault Lines in China's Economic Terrain*, p 17.

[5] Cited in above.

[6] As above.

[7] Yu Jianrong, *Significant Shift in Focus of Peasants' Rights Activism*, Chinese Academy of Social Sciences, 19 December, 2005.

[8] Reported in *Xinhua*, 17 March, 2006.

[9] For example, see Charles Wolf Jr. et al, *Fault Lines in China's Economic Terrain*; Gordon G. Chang, *The Coming Collapse of China*.

[10] Zhu Qingfang, 'Worries about the livelihood of urban and rural residents in the year 2001), *Reform Internal Reference* (6, 2002), p 30-1.

[11] See Valerie Hudson & Andrea den Boer, *Bare Branches: The Security Implications of Asia's Surplus Male Population* (Cambridge: The MIT Press, 2004). There are 117 males for every 100 females in China. The global average is about 105:100.

[12] *China Statistical Yearbook 2000* (Beijing: Government Press, 2001).

[13] As above.

[14] Yasheng Huang, 'Institutional Environment and Private Sector Development in China,' Asia Program Special Report, *Woodrow Wilson International Centre for Scholars*, July, 2005, p 27-8.

[15] Above, p 29-30.

[16] Chenghui Zhang, 'Research Report on the current Financing Situation of Privately-owned Enterprises,' *China Development*

Review (3:3, 2001), p 82.

[17] *China Statistical Yearbook 2000.*

[18] Xun Zi, 'Enterprise Overhaul Needed to rise to WTO Challenge,' *China Daily,* 6 August, 2001.

[19] Zhang Hanya, Secretary-General of China Investment Association, cited in Thomas Rawski, 'China's Growth Prospects', *Asia Program Special Report* (Pittsburg: University of Pittsburg, 2005), p 57.

[20] John Giles, Albert Park and Fang Cai, 'How has Economic Restructuring Affected China's Urban Workers?,' *The China Quarterly* (185, 2006), p 87.

[21] For example, see Minxin Pei, *China's Trapped Transition*, p 199-200.

[22] As above.

[23] State Council Development Research Centre, 'The Medical Reform Controversy,' *Beijing Review* (48: 38, 2005).

[24] Minxin Pei, *China's Trapped Transition,*, p 173.

[25] See www.chinanews.com.cn, December 3, 2004.

[26] Charles Wolf Jr. et al, *Fault Lines in China's Economic Terrain,* p 53.

[27] Emmanuel Pitsilis, David A. von Emloh, and Yi Wang, 'Filling China's Pension Gap,' *McKinsey Quarterly* (2, 2002).

[28] Alastair Newton and Robert Subbaraman, 'China: Gigantic Possibilities, Present Realities,' *Lehman Brothers Research Report*, 21 January 2002, p. 69.

[29] Peiyen Zeng (ed.), *New China's Economy in the Last Fifty Years, 1949-1999*, (Beijing: China Planning Press, 1999), p 632.

[30] World Bank, *China: Overcoming Rural Poverty* (Washington DC: World Bank, 2001), p 2. Official Chinese figures use the figure of less than US0.66 per day as the poverty standard. The international standard is US1.00 per day.

[31] Cited in Minxin Pei,' Creeping Democratisation in China,' *Journal of Democracy* (6:4, 1995), p 73.

[32] The surveys are based on research done by Pei: see Minxin Pei, *China's Trapped Transition*, p 184.

33 From Li Jing and Cheng Wei, 'An Investigation into the Management of Party Members in Enterprises That Have Ceased or Partially Ceased Operation', *Party-Building Research* (2, 1998), p 38.

34 Research cited in Minxin Pei, *China's Trapped Transition*, p 185.

35 Cited in above, p 187-8.

36 'Unrest' is simply defined as 'big' disturbances by the officials.

37 Reported in http://www.gov.cn, 19 January 2006.

38 Dexter Roberts, 'China: A Workers' State Helping the Workers?', *Business Week*, 13 December 2004; David Murphy, 'The Dangers of Too Much Success,' *Far Eastern Economic Review*, 10 June 2004.

39 Thomas Lum, 'Social Unrest in China', *CRS Report for Congress*, 8 May 8 2006, p 1.

40 See Ministry of Civil Affairs' statement in 'China bans Falun Gong', *People's Daily*, 22 July 1999.

41 See Banning Garrett, 'China Debates the Contradictions of Globalisation', *Asian Survey* (41:3, 2001). p 412.

42 See Josh Kurlantzick, 'China's Repressed Memory of the Cultural Revolution: Silent Revolution,' *The New Republic*, 18 September, 2006.

43 Quoted in above.

44 The estimate is a conservative one is most likely to be above this number of people: see Carolyn Bartholomew, *China: Cooperation or Competition?* (Taiwan: Asia-Pacific Affairs Forum – China Series, August 15, 2006), p 5.

45 Cited in Minxin Pei, *China's Trapped Transition,* p 188.

46 Michael Elliott, 'Small World, Big Stakes,' *Time*, 19 June, 2005.

47 Deng Xiaoping, *Selected Works of Deng Xiaoping, 1975-1982*, (Beijing: Renmin, 1983), p 301.

48 Hu Jintao, 'Speech commemorating the 50th anniversary of the founding of the National Peoples' Congress' (September 15, 2004): http://english.people.cn//200409/15/

eng20040915_157073.html

Part B Chapter 1

1   Zheng Bijian, 'China's 'Peaceful Rise' to Great Power Status', *Foreign Affairs* (September/October, 2005).

2   Kishore Mahbubani, 'Understanding China', *Foreign Affairs* (September/October, 2005).

3   Quoted in Esther Pan, 'The promise and pitfalls of China's 'Peaceful Rise',' Council on Foreign Relations, 14 April, 2006: http://www.cfr.org/publication/10446

4   Robert Conquest, *The Dragons of Expectation* (London: Gerald Duckworth & Co, 2006).

5   Albert Keidel, *China's Internal Unrest*, Written testimony before the US-China Economic and Security Review Commission, 2 February, 2006.

6   Alfred B. Evans, *Soviet Marxism-Leninism: The Decline of an Ideology* (Westport: Praeger, 1993).

7   See Paul Mooney, 'China faces up to growing unrest,' *Asia Times*, 16 November, 2004.

8   *A Health Situation Assessment of the PRC* (New York: UN, July 2005).

9   See Statement by Dr. Joshua Muldavin, *Major Internal Challenges Facing the Chinese Leadership*, US-China Economic and Security Review Commission, 2-3 February, 2006.

10   See Wu Chuntao and Chen Guidi (trans., Zuo Hong), *Will the Boat Sink the Water?: The Life of China's Peasants* (New York: Pacific Affairs, 2006).

11   See Paul Mooney, 'China faces up to growing unrest.'

12   See Albert Keidel, *China's Internal Unrest*.

13   See Dr. Murray Scott Tanner, 'Chinese Government Responses to Rising Social Unrest', *China's State Controlled Mechanisms and Methods*, US-China Economic and Security Review Commission, 14 April, 2005.

14   *China Human Development Report 2005* (Beijing: UNDP, 2005).

15 *China's Optimism*, Pew Global Attitudes Project, 11
    November, 2005: http://pewglobal.org/reports/display.
    php?ReportID=249

16 See David Kelly, 'Social Movements in Urban China,'
    ChinaBrief (VI:2, 20 January, 2006).

17 Pepe Escobar, 'The peasant Tiananmen time bomb,' *Asia
    Times*, 22 January, 2005.

18 Quoted in Philip Pan, 'Civil Unrest Challenges China's Party
    Leadership,' *Washington Post*, 4 November, 2004,, p A18.

19 Dr. Murray Scott Tanner, 'Chinese Government Responses
    to Rising Social Unrest', p 129.

20 As above, p 131.

21 See Larry M. Wortzel, 'The Tiananmen Massacre
    Reappraised,' in *Chinese Security Decision Making Under
    Stress*, ed. Andrew Scobell & Larry M. Wortzel (Washington
    DC: Strategic Studies Institute, 2005) for an analysis of the
    indecision and paralysis that gripped the senior leadership
    leading up to and during the Tiananmen crisis.

22 China News Service, 6 March, 2006: http://www.jamestown.
    org/news_details.php?news_id=172

23 Jane Macartney, 'Mr Who? The man of mystery who controls
    more than a billion people,' *The Times*, 5 November, 2005.

24 See Willy Lam, 'Hu's Campaign for Ideological Purity,'
    China Brief (5:2, 2005).

25 Cited in above.

26 For example, General Liu Yuan, son of former state
    president Liu Shaoqi, was promoted Political Commissar
    of the Academy of Military Sciences, while General Zhang
    Haiyang, the son of retired general and former Politburo
    member Zhang Zhen, was made Political Commissar of the
    important Chengdu Military Region.

27 Cited in Willy Lam, 'Hu's Campaign for Ideological Purity'.

28 *People's Daily*, 5 January, 2005.

29 Mao Tse-tung, Problems of War and Strategy', *Selected
    Works,* Vol. II, 1938 (Peking: Foreign Languages Press,
    1967), p 224.

[30] Reported in *Xinhua*, 29 September, 2005.

[31] Some experts like Cheng Hsiao-shih argued that Party control has never been institutionalised at all: *Party-Military Relations in the PRC and Taiwan* (Boulder; Westview Press, 1990).

[32] The Gini coefficient measuring income inequality has worsened by 50 percent from 20 years ago.

[33] Admiral Liu Huaqing and Zhang Zhen, quoted in Andrew Scobell, 'China's Evolving Civil-Military Relations,' *Armed Forces & Society* (31:2, 2005), p 232-3.

[34] For example, following the 10th National People's Congress, one PLA delegate, Major General Ding Jiye, complained publicly that the new military budget was 'barely enough to keep things moving.': 'Major General Ding Jiye Says Defense Spending Much Lower Than World Average,' *Xinhua*, 8 March, 2003. With respect to involvement in politics, numerous Generals were publicly siding either with then CMC Chairman Jiang Zemin or President Hu who was then the Vice-Chairman of the CMC.

[35] See Willy Lam, 'Beijing's Great Leap Outward: Power Projection with Chinese Characteristics,' *Jamestown China Brief* (8 February, 2007).

[36] Quoted in Willy Lo-Lap Lam, 'China Preparing for Future Fight With US,' *CNN Report*, 27 March, 2003.

[37] Quoted in above.

Part B Chapter 2

[1] George T. Crane, 'China's Democratic Prospects: A Dissenting View,' in *China in The National Interest*, ed. Owen Harries (London: Transaction Publishers, 2003), p 142.

[2] See Eric Cheow, 'Paying Tribute To Beijing,' *International Herald Tribune*, 21 January, 2004.

[3] Suisheng Zhao, 'China's Pragmatic Nationalism: Is It Manageable?', *Washington Quarterly* (29:1, 2005), p 132-3.

[4] Peter Gries, *China's New Nationalism* (Berkeley: University of California Press, 1994), p 12.

[5] See Joshua Kurlantzick, 'China's chance', *Prospect Magazine*

(Issue 108, March 2005).

6   Pew Global Attitudes Project, *China's Neighbours Worry About Its Growing Military Strength*, 21 September, 2006. Contrast this with respondents from Russia, India and Japan where 76, 63, and 93 percent respectively viewed China's rising military strength as a 'Bad Thing'.

7   Quoted in Joshua Kurlantzick, 'China's chance'.

8   Dr. Joshua Muldavin, *Statement to U.S.-China Economic and Security Review Commission*, 2-3 February, 2006, p 111.

9   See John Pomfret, 'New Nationalism Drives Beijing,' *Washington Post*, 4 April, 2001, p A1.

10   Edward Friedman, Chinese nationalism: challenge to US interests,' in *The People's Liberation Army and China in Transition*, ed. Stephen J. Flanagan & Michael E. Marti (Washington DC: National Defence University, 2003).

11   Suisheng Zhao, 'China's Pragmatic Nationalism: Is It Manageable?', p 132.

12   See Nan Li, 'PLA Conservative Nationalism,' in ed. Stephen J. Flanagan & Michael E. Marti.

13   Evan A. Feigenbaum, 'China's Challenge to *Pax Americana*', *Washington Quarterly* (Summer 2001), p 32-3.

14   Thomas J. Christensen, 'The Contemporary Security Dilemma: Deterring a Taiwan Conflict,' *Washington Quarterly* (25:4, 2002), p 13.

15   See Joseph Kahn, 'Chinese Officers Say Taiwan's Leaders Are Near Abyss of War,' *New York Times*, 4 December, 2003.

16   Richard Bush, 'Chinese Decision Making Under Stress,' in ed. Andrew Scobell & Larry M. Wortzel, 'China's Evolving Civil-Military Relations', p 135-60.

17   See Dr. Eric Cheow, 'Rising Chinese Nationalism and the Taiwan Question,' *China Brief*, 15 April, 2004, p 3.

18   See Avery Goldstein, *Rising to the Challenge: China's Grand Strategy and International Security* (Stanford: Stanford University Press, 2005), p 95-6.

19   Willy Lam, 'Beijing's Great Leap Outward'.

20   See Joshua Kurlantzick, 'China's chance'.

21 For example, see Henry Kissinger, 'Conflict is not an option,' *International Herald Tribune*, 9 June, 2005.

22 James Mann, *The China Fantasy: How Our Leaders Explain Away Chinese Repression* (Viking 2007).

23 Robert Kagan, 'The Illusion of 'Managing' China,' *The Washington Post*, 15 May, 2005.

24 As above.

25 Thomas J. Christensen (Deputy Assistant Secretary for East Asian and Pacific Affairs), 'China's role in the world: Is China a 'Responsible Stakeholder'?' addressing the U.S.-China Economic & Security Review Commission (Washington DC: August 3, 2006).

Part B Chapter 3

1   John Fitzgerald, 'China and the Quest for Dignity,' The National Interest (55, 1999)

2   Ross Terrill, 'The myth of the rise of China', *The Australian* (September 19, 2005.)

INDEX